# CHANGE
# BY
# DESIGN

HOW DESIGN THINKING
TRANSFORMS ORGANIZATIONS
AND INSPIRES INNOVATION

# CHANGE

# BY

# DESIGN

## TIM BROWN

### WITH BARRY KATZ

HARPER
BUSINESS

*An Imprint of* HarperCollins*Publishers*
www.harpercollins.com

HarperCollins books may be purchased for educational, business, or sales promotional use. For information, please e-mail the Special Markets Department at SPsales@harpercollins.com.

FIRST EDITION

*Designed by William Ruoto*

Library of Congress Cataloging-in-Publication Data

Brown, Tim.
    Change by design: how design thinking transforms organizations and inspires innovation / Tim Brown.—1st ed.
        p.   cm.
Includes index.
    ISBN 978-0-06-176608-4
    1. Organizational change. 2. Industrial design. I. Title.
HD58.8.B772   2009
658.4'063—dc22                                                2009014596

15 16   OV/RRD   30 29 28 27

*To Gaynor*

# CONTENTS

# the power of design thinking

## an end to old ideas

Practically everyone who has visited England has experienced the Great Western Railway, the crowning achievement of the great Victorian engineer Isambard Kingdom Brunel. I grew up within earshot of the GWR, and as a child in rural Oxfordshire I often bicycled alongside the line and waited for the great express trains to roar past at more than one hundred miles an hour. The train ride is more comfortable today (the carriages now sport springs and cushioned seats) and the scenery has certainly changed, but a century and a half after it was built the GWR still stands as an icon of the industrial revolution— and as an example of the power of design to shape the world around us.

Although he was the engineer's engineer, Brunel was not solely interested in the technology behind his creations. While considering the design of the system, he insisted upon the flattest possible gradient because he wanted passengers to have the sense of "floating across the countryside." He constructed bridges, viaducts, cuttings, and tunnels all in the cause of creating not just efficient transportation but the best possible experience. He even imagined an integrated transport system that would allow the traveler to board a train at London's Paddington Station and disembark from a steamship in New York. In every one of his great projects Brunel displayed a remarkable—and remarkably prescient—talent for balancing technical, commercial, and human considerations. He was not just a great engineer or a gifted designer; Isambard Kingdom Brunel was one of the earliest examples of a *design thinker*.

Since the completion of the Great Western Railway in 1841, industrialization has wrought incredible change. Technology has helped lift millions out of poverty and has improved the standard of living of a considerable portion of humanity. As we enter the twenty-first century, however, we are increasingly aware of the underside of the revolution that has transformed the way we live, work, and play. The sooty clouds of smoke that once darkened the skies over Manchester and Birmingham have changed the climate of the planet. The torrent of cheap goods that began to flow from their factories and workshops has fed into a culture of excess consumption and prodigious waste. The industrialization of agriculture has left us vulnerable to natural and man-made catastrophes. The innovative breakthroughs of the past have become the routine procedures of today as businesses in Shenzhen and Bangalore tap into the same management theories as those in Silicon Valley and Detroit and face the same downward spiral of commoditization.

Technology still has not run its course. The communications revolution sparked by the Internet has brought people closer together and given them the opportunity to share perspectives and create new ideas as never before. The sciences of biology, chemistry, and physics have merged in the forms of biotechnology and nanotechnology to create the promise of lifesaving medicines and wondrous new materials. But these spectacular achievements are unlikely to help us reverse our ominous course. Just the opposite.

## we need new choices

A purely technocentric view of innovation is less sustainable now than ever, and a management philosophy based only on selecting from existing strategies is likely to be overwhelmed by new developments at home or abroad. What we need are new choices—new products that balance the needs of individuals and of society as a whole; new ideas that tackle the global challenges of health, poverty, and education; new strategies that result in differences that matter and a sense of purpose that engages everyone affected by them. It is hard to imagine a time when the challenges we faced so vastly exceeded the creative resources we have brought to bear on them. Aspiring innovators may have attended a "brainstorming" session or learned a few gimmicks and tricks, but rarely do these temporary placeholders make it to the outside world in the form of new products, services, or strategies.

What we need is an approach to innovation that is powerful, effective, and broadly accessible, that can be integrated into all aspects of business and society, and that individuals and teams can use to generate breakthrough ideas that are implemented and that therefore have an impact. Design thinking, the subject of this book, offers just such an approach.

Design thinking begins with skills designers have learned over many decades in their quest to match human needs with available technical resources within the practical constraints of business. By integrating what is desirable from a human point of view with what is technologically feasible and economically viable, designers have been able to create the products we enjoy today. Design thinking takes the next step, which is to put these tools into the hands of people who may have never thought of themselves as designers and apply them to a vastly greater range of problems.

Design thinking taps into capacities we all have but that are overlooked by more conventional problem-solving practices. It is not only human-centered; it is deeply human in and of itself. Design thinking relies on our ability to be intuitive, to recognize patterns, to construct ideas that have emotional meaning as well as functionality, to express ourselves in media other than words or symbols. Nobody wants to run a business based on feeling, intuition, and inspiration, but an overreliance on the rational and the analytical can be just as dangerous. The integrated approach at the core of the design process suggests a "third way."

## swimming upstream

I was trained as an industrial designer, but it took me a long time to realize the difference between *being* a designer and *thinking like* a designer. Seven years of undergraduate and graduate education and fifteen years of professional practice went by before I had any real inkling that what I was doing was more than simply a link in a chain that connected a client's engineering department to the folks upstairs in marketing.

The very first products I designed as a design professional were for a venerable English machinery manufacturer called Wadkin Bursgreen. The people there invited a young and untested industrial designer into their midst to help improve their professional woodworking machines. I spent a summer creating drawings and models of circular saws that were better looking and spindle molders that were easier to use. I think I did a pretty good job, and it's still possible to find my work in factories thirty years later. But you will no longer find the Wadkin Bursgreen company, which has long since gone out of business. As a designer I didn't see that it was the future of the woodworking industry that was in question, not the design of its machines.

Only gradually did I come to see the power of design not as a link in a chain but as the hub of a wheel. When I left the protected world of art school—where everyone looked the same, acted the same, and spoke the same language—and entered the world of business, I had to spend far more time trying to explain to my clients what design was than actually doing it. I realized that I was approaching the world from a set of operating principles that was different from theirs. The resulting confusion was getting in the way of my creativity and productivity.

I also noticed that the people who inspired me were not necessarily members of the design profession: engineers such as Isambard Kingdom Brunel, Thomas Edison, and Ferdinand Porsche, all of whom seemed to have a human-centered rather than technology-centered worldview; behavioral scientists such as Don Norman, who asked why products are so needlessly confusing; artists such as Andy Goldsworthy and Antony Gormley, who seemed to engage their viewers in an experience that made them part of the artwork; business leaders such as Steve Jobs and Akio Morita, who were creating unique and meaningful products. I realized that behind the soaring rhetoric of "genius" and "visionary" was a basic commitment to the principles of design thinking.

A few years ago, during one of the periodic booms and busts that are part of business as usual in Silicon Valley, my colleagues and I were struggling to figure how to keep my company, IDEO, meaningful and useful in the world. There was plenty of interest in our design services, but we also noticed that we were increasingly being asked to tackle problems that seemed very far away from the commonly held view of design. A health care foundation was asking us to help restructure its organization; a century-old manufacturing company was asking us to help it better understand its clients; an elite university was asking us to think about alternative learning environments. We were being pulled out of our comfort zone, but this was exciting because it opened up new possibilities for us to have more impact in the world.

We started to talk about this expanded field as "design with a small d" in an attempt to move beyond the sculptural *objet* displayed in lifestyle magazines or on pedestals in museums of modern art. But this phrase never seemed fully satisfactory. One day I was chatting with my friend David Kelley, a Stanford professor and the founder of IDEO, and he remarked that every time someone came to ask him about design, he found himself inserting the word "thinking" to explain what it was that designers do. The term "design thinking" stuck. I now use it as a way of describing a set of principles that can be applied by diverse people to a wide range of problems. I have become a convert and an evangelist of design thinking.

And I am not alone. Today, rather than enlist designers to make an already developed idea more attractive, the most progressive companies are challenging them to create ideas at the outset of the development process. The former role is tactical; it builds on what exists and usually moves it one step further. The latter is strategic; it pulls "design" out of the studio and unleashes its disruptive, game-changing potential. It's no accident that designers can now be found in the boardrooms of some of the world's most progressive companies. As a thought process, design has begun to move upstream.

Moreover, the principles of design thinking turn out to be applicable to a wide range of organizations, not just to companies in search of new product offerings. A competent designer can always improve upon last year's new widget, but an interdisciplinary team of skilled design thinkers is in a position to tackle more complex problems. From pediatric obesity to crime prevention to climate change, design thinking is now being applied to a range of challenges that bear little resemblance to the covetable objects that fill the pages of today's coffee-table publications.

The causes underlying the growing interest in design are clear. As the center of economic activity in the developing world shifts inexorably from industrial manufacturing to knowledge creation and service delivery, innovation has become nothing less than a survival strategy. It is, moreover, no longer limited to the introduction of new physical products but includes new sorts of processes, services, interactions, entertainment forms, and ways of communicating and collaborating. These are exactly the kinds of human-centered tasks that designers work on every day. The natural evolution from *design doing* to *design thinking* reflects the growing recognition on the part of today's business leaders that design has become too important to be left to designers.

*Change by Design* is divided into two parts. The first is a journey through some of the important stages of design thinking. It is not intended as a "how-to" guide, for ultimately these are skills best acquired through doing. What I hope to do is to provide a framework that will help the reader identify the principles and practices that make for great design thinking. As I suggest in chapter 6, design thinking flourishes in a rich culture of storytelling, and in that spirit I will explore many of these ideas by telling stories drawn from IDEO and other companies and organizations.

The first part of the book focuses on design thinking as applied to business. Along the way we will see how it has been practiced by some of the most innovative companies in the world, how it has inspired breakthrough solutions, and where, on occasion, it has overreached (any business book that claims an unbroken record of success belongs on the "fiction" shelf). Part two is intended as a challenge for all of us to Think Big. By looking at three broad domains of human activity—business, markets, and society—I hope to show how design thinking can be extended in new ways to create ideas that are equal to the challenges we all face. If you are managing a hotel, design thinking can help you to rethink the very nature of hospitality.

If you are working with a philanthropic agency, design thinking can help you grasp the needs of the people you are trying to serve. If you are a venture capitalist, design thinking can help you peer into the future.

## another way to look at it

Ben Loehnen, my excellent editor at Harper Business, advised me that a proper book needs a proper table of contents. I have done my best to oblige. The truth is, however, that I see things a bit differently. Design thinking is all about exploring different possibilities, so I thought I would start by introducing the reader to another way of visualizing the contents of the book. There are times when linear thinking is called for, but at IDEO we often find it more helpful to visualize an idea using a technique with a long, rich history, the mind map.

Linear thinking is about sequences; mind maps are about connections. This visual representation helps me see the relationships between the different topics I want to talk about, it gives me a more intuitive sense of the whole, and it helps me to think about how best to illustrate an idea. Linear thinkers like Ben are welcome to use the table of contents; more venturesome readers may wish to consult the inside cover and view the whole of *Change by Design* in one place. It may prompt you to jump to a particular section of interest. It may help you retrace your steps. It may remind you of the relationships among different topics of design thinking and may even help you to think of topics that are not covered here but should be.

Experienced design thinkers may find that the mind map is

all you need to capture my point of view. I hope that for everyone else the ten chapters that follow will provide a worthwhile insight into the world of design thinking and the potential it has for us to create meaningful change. If that proves to be the case, I hope you will let me know.

TIM BROWN
*Palo Alto, California, May 2009*

# PART I

## what is design thinking?

# getting under your skin,
## or *how design thinking is about more than style*

I n 2004 Shimano, a leading Japanese manufacturer of bicycle components, was experiencing flattening growth in
its traditional high-end road racing and mountain bike seg-
ments in the United States. The company had always relied on
new technology to drive its growth. It had invested heavily in
an effort to anticipate the next innovation. In the face of the
changing market it seemed prudent to try something new, so
Shimano invited IDEO to collaborate.

What followed was an exercise in designer-client relations
that looked very different from what such an engagement
might have looked like a few decades or even a few years earlier. Shimano did not hand us a list of technical specifications
and a binder full of market research and send us off to design a
bunch of parts. Rather, we joined forces and set out together to
explore the changing terrain of the cycling market.

During the initial phase, we fielded an interdisciplinary team
of designers, behavioral scientists, marketers, and engineers whose
task was to identify appropriate constraints for the project. The
team began with a hunch that it should not focus on the high-
end market. Instead, they fanned out to learn why 90 percent of
American adults don't ride bikes—despite the fact that 90 percent
of them did as kids! Looking for new ways to think about the
problem, they spent time with consumers from across the spec-

trum. They discovered that nearly everyone they met had happy memories of being a kid on a bike but many are deterred by cycling today—by the retail experience (including the intimidating, Lycra-clad athletes who serve as sales staff in most independent bike stores); by the bewildering complexity and excessive cost of the bikes, accessories, and specialized clothing; by the danger of cycling on roads not designed for bicycles; and by the demands of maintaining a sophisticated machine that might be ridden only on weekends. They noted that everyone they talked to seemed to have a bike in the garage with a flat tire or a broken cable.

This human-centered exploration—which looked for insights from bicycle aficionados but also, more important, from people outside Shimano's core customer base—led to the realization that a whole new category of bicycling might reconnect American consumers to their experiences as children. A huge, untapped market began to take shape before their eyes.

The design team, inspired by the old Schwinn coaster bikes that everyone seemed to remember, came up with the concept of "coasting." Coasting would entice lapsed bikers back into an activity that was simple, straightforward, healthy, and fun. Coasting bikes, built more for pleasure than for sport, would have no controls on the handlebars, no cables snaking along the frame, no nest of precision gears to be cleaned, adjusted, repaired, and replaced. As we remember from our earliest bikes, the brakes would be applied by backpedaling. Coasting bikes would feature comfortable padded seats, upright handlebars, and puncture-resistant tires and require almost no maintenance. But this is not simply a retrobike: it incorporates sophisticated engineering with an automatic transmission that shifts the gears as the bicycle gains speed or slows.

Three major manufacturers—Trek, Raleigh, and Giant—began to develop new bikes incorporating innovative components from Shimano, but the team didn't stop there. *Designers* might have ended the project with the bike itself, but as holistic *design thinkers* they pressed ahead. They created in-store retailing strategies for independent bike dealers, in part to mitigate the discomfort that novices felt in retail settings built to serve enthusiasts. The team developed a brand that identified coasting as a way to enjoy life ("Chill. Explore. Dawdle. Lollygag. First one there's a rotten egg."). In collaboration with local governments and cycling organizations, it designed a public relations campaign including a Web site that identified safe places to ride.

Many other people and organizations became involved in the project as it passed from inspiration through ideation and on into the implementation phase. Remarkably, the first problem the designers would have been expected to address—the look of the bikes—was deferred to a late stage in the development process, when the team created a "reference design" to show what was possible and to inspire the bicycle manufacturers' own design teams. Within a year of the bike's successful launch, seven more manufacturers had signed up to produce coasting bikes. An exercise in design had become an exercise in design thinking.

## three spaces of innovation

Although I would love to provide a simple, easy-to-follow recipe that would ensure that every project ends as successfully as this one, the nature of design thinking makes that impossible. In contrast to the champions of scientific management at the beginning of the last century, design thinkers know that there is no "one best way" to move through the process. There are useful starting points and helpful landmarks along the way, but the continuum of innovation is best thought of as a system of overlapping spaces rather than a sequence of orderly steps. We can think of them as *inspiration*, the problem or opportunity that motivates the search for solutions; *ideation*, the process of generating, developing, and testing ideas; and *implementation*, the path that leads from the project room to the market. Projects may loop back through these spaces more than once as the team refines its ideas and explores new directions.

The reason for the iterative, nonlinear nature of the journey is not that design thinkers are disorganized or undisciplined but that design thinking is fundamentally an exploratory process; done right, it will invariably make unexpected discoveries along the way, and it would be foolish not to find out where they lead. Often these discoveries can be integrated into the ongoing process without disruption. At other times the discovery will motivate the team to revisit some of its most basic assumptions. While testing a prototype, for instance, consumers may provide us with insights that point to a more interesting, more promising, and potentially more profitable market opening up in front of us. Insights of this sort should inspire us to refine or rethink our assumptions rather than press onward in adherence to an original plan. To borrow the language of the computer industry, this approach should be seen not as a system reset but as a meaningful upgrade.

The risk of such an iterative approach is that it appears to extend the time it takes to get an idea to market, but this is often a shortsighted perception. To the contrary, a team that understands what is happening will not feel bound to take the next logical step along an ultimately unproductive path. We have seen many projects killed by management because it became clear that the ideas were not good enough. When a project is terminated after months or even years, it can be devastating in terms of both money and morale. A nimble team of design thinkers will have been prototyping from day one and self-correcting along the way. As we say at IDEO, "Fail early to succeed sooner."

Insofar as it is open-ended, open-minded, and iterative, a process fed by design thinking will feel chaotic to those experiencing it for the first time. But over the life of a project, it invariably comes to make sense and achieves results that differ markedly from the linear, milestone-based processes that define traditional business practices. In any case, predictability leads to boredom and boredom leads to the loss of talented people. It also leads to results that rivals find easy to copy. It is better to take an experimental approach: share processes, encourage the collective ownership of ideas, and enable teams to learn from one another.

A second way to think about the overlapping spaces of innovation is in terms of boundaries. To an artist in pursuit of beauty or a scientist in search of truth, the bounds of a project may appear as unwelcome constraints. But the mark of a designer, as the legendary Charles Eames said often, is a willing embrace of constraints.

Without constraints design cannot happen, and the best design—a precision medical device or emergency shelter for disaster victims—is often carried out within quite severe constraints. For less extreme cases we need only look at Target's success in bringing design within the reach of a broader population for significantly less cost than had previously been achieved. It is actually much more difficult for an accomplished designer such as Michael Graves to create a collection of low-cost kitchen implements or Isaac Mizrahi a line of ready-to-wear clothing than it is to design a teakettle that will sell in a museum store for hundreds of dollars or a dress that will sell in a boutique for thousands.

The willing and even enthusiastic acceptance of competing constraints is the foundation of design thinking. The first stage of the design process is often about discovering which constraints are important and establishing a framework for evaluating them. Constraints can best be visualized in terms of three overlapping criteria for successful ideas: feasibility (what is functionally possible within the foreseeable future); viability (what is likely to become part of a sustainable business model); and desirability (what makes sense to people and for people).

A competent designer will resolve each of these three constraints, but a *design thinker* will bring them into a harmonious balance. The popular Nintendo Wii is a good example of what happens when someone gets it right. For many years a veritable arms race of more sophisticated graphics and more expensive consoles has been driving the gaming industry. Nintendo realized that it would be possible to break out of this vicious circle—and create a more immersive experience—by using the new technology of gestural control. This meant less focus on the resolution of the screen graphics, which in turn led to a less expensive console and better margins on the product. The Wii

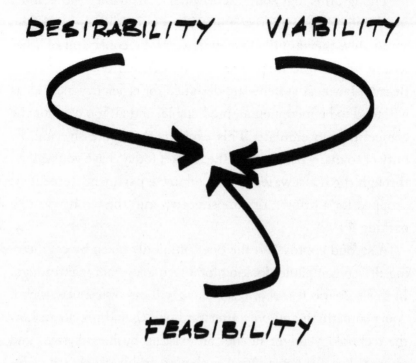

DESIRABILITY     VIABILITY

FEASIBILITY

strikes a perfect balance of desirability, feasibility, and viability. It has created a more engaging user experience and generated huge profits for Nintendo.

This pursuit of peaceful coexistence does not imply that all constraints are created equal; a given project may be driven disproportionately by technology, budget, or a volatile mix of human factors. Different types of organizations may push one or another of them to the fore. Nor is it a simple linear process. Design teams will cycle back through all three considerations throughout the life of a project, but the emphasis on fundamental human needs—as distinct from fleeting or artificially manipulated desires—is what drives design thinking to depart from the status quo.

Though this may sound self-evident, the reality is that most companies tend to approach new ideas quite differently. Quite reasonably, they are likely to start with the constraint of what will fit within the framework of the existing business model. Because business systems are designed for efficiency, new ideas will tend to be incremental, predictable, and all too easy for the competition to emulate. This explains the oppressive uniformity of so many products on the market today; have you walked through the housewares section of any department store lately, shopped for a printer, or almost gotten into the wrong car in a parking lot?

A second approach is the one commonly taken by engineering-driven companies looking for a technological breakthrough. In this scenario teams of researchers will discover a new way of doing something and only afterward will they think about how the technology might fit into an existing business system and create value. As Peter Drucker showed in his classic study *Innovation and Entrepreneurship*, reliance on technology is hugely risky. Relatively few technical innovations bring an immediate economic benefit that will justify the investments of time and resources they require. This may explain the steady decline of the large corporate R&D labs such as Xerox PARC and Bell Labs that were such powerful incubators in the 1960s and '70s. Today, corporations instead attempt to narrow their innovation efforts to ideas that have more near-term business potential. They may be making a big mistake. By focusing their attention on near-term viability, they may be trading innovation for increment.

Finally, an organization may be driven by its estimation of basic human needs and desires. At its worst this may mean dreaming up alluring but essentially meaningless products destined for the local landfill—persuading people, in the blunt words of the design gadfly Victor Papanek, "to buy things they don't need with money they don't have to impress neighbors who don't care." Even when the goals are laudable, however—moving travelers safely through a security checkpoint or delivering clean water to rural communities in impoverished countries—the primary focus on one element of the triad of constraints, rather than the appropriate balance among all three, may undermine the sustainability of the overall program.

## the project

Designers, then, have learned to excel at resolving one or another or even all three of these constraints. *Design thinkers*, by contrast, are learning to navigate between and among them in creative ways. They do so because they have shifted their thinking from *problem* to *project*.

The project is the vehicle that carries an idea from concept to reality. Unlike many other processes we are used to—from playing the piano to paying our bills—a design project is not open-ended and ongoing. It has a beginning, a middle, and an end, and it is precisely these restrictions that anchor it to the real world. That design thinking is expressed within the context of a project forces us to articulate a clear goal at the outset. It creates natural deadlines that impose discipline and give us an opportunity to review progress, make midcourse corrections, and redirect future activity. The clarity, direction, and limits of a well-defined project are vital to sustaining a high level of creative energy.

The "Innovate or Die Pedal-Powered Machine Contest" competition is a good example. Google teamed up with the bike company Specialized to create a design competition whose modest challenge was to use bicycle technology to change the world. The winning team—five committed designers and an extended family of enthusiastic supporters—was a late starter. In a few frenzied weeks of brainstorming and prototyping, the team was able to identify a pressing issue (1.1 billion people in developing countries do not have access to clean drinking water), explore a variety of alternative solutions (mobile or stationary? trailer or luggage rack?) and build a working prototype: The Aquaduct, a human-powered tricycle designed to filter drinking water while transporting it, is now traveling the world to help promote clean water innovation. It succeeded because of the inflexible constraints of technology (pedal power), budget ($0.00), and inflexible deadline. The experience of the Aquaduct team is the reverse of that found in most academic or corporate labs, where the objective may be to extend the life of a research project indefinitely and where the end of a project may mean nothing more than the funding has dried up.

## the brief

The classic starting point of any project is the brief. Almost like a scientific hypothesis, the brief is a set of mental constraints that gives the project team a framework from which to begin, benchmarks by which they can measure progress, and a set of objectives to be realized: price point, available technology, market segment, and so on. The analogy goes even further.

Just as a hypothesis is not the same as an algorithm, the project brief is not a set of instructions or an attempt to answer a question before it has been posed. Rather, a well-constructed brief will allow for serendipity, unpredictability, and the capricious whims of fate, for that is the creative realm from which breakthrough ideas emerge. If you already know what you are after, there is usually not much point in looking.

When I first started practicing as an industrial designer, the brief was handed to us in an envelope. It usually took the form of a highly constrained set of parameters that left us with little more to do than wrap a more or less attractive shell around a product whose basic concept had already been decided elsewhere. One of my first assignments was to design a new personal fax machine for a Danish electronics manufacturer. The technical aspects of the product took the form of a set of components that were being supplied by another company. Its commercial viability had been established by "management" and was geared to an existing market. Even its desirability had largely been predetermined by precedent, as everybody supposedly knew what a fax machine was supposed to look like. There was not a lot of room for maneuver, and I was left to try to make the machine stand out against those of other designers who were trying to do the same thing. It is no wonder that as more companies mastered the game, the competition among them became ever more intense. Nor have things changed much over the years. As one frustrated client recently lamented, "We are busting our ass for a few tenths of a percent of market share." The erosion of margin and value is the inevitable result.

The proof of this can be found at any consumer electronics store, where, under the buzz of the fluorescent lights, thousands

of products are arrayed on the shelves, clamoring for our attention and differentiated only by unnecessary if not unfathom-
able features. Gratuitous efforts at styling and assertive graphics and packaging may catch our eye but do little to enhance
the experience of ownership and use. A design brief that is too
abstract risks leaving the project team wandering about in a fog.
One that starts from too narrow a set of constraints, however,
almost guarantees that the outcome will be incremental and,
most likely, mediocre. It transfers to the design realm what
economists like to call "the race to the bottom." Not for nothing did its founders call economics "the dismal science."

The art of the brief can raise the bar and set great organizations apart from moderately successful ones. Procter & Gamble is a good example. In 2002 the company embarked on an
initiative to use design as a source of innovation and growth.
Driven by Chief Innovation Officer Claudia Kotchka, each
of P&G's divisions began to add design-led innovation to the
strong technical R&D efforts for which the company was justly
famous.

Karl Ronn, the head of R&D for P&G's Home Care Division, was one of the first senior executives to see the potential of
this approach. His stated goal was not to produce incremental
additions to existing products and brands but to inspire innovation that would generate significant growth. This led him to
IDEO with a brief that was the ideal mix of freedom and constraint: reinvent bathroom cleaning with an emphasis on what
was enigmatically called "the everyday clean." Ronn didn't
show up with the latest technology from the lab and instruct
the team to package it in streamlines and tail fins. He didn't ask
us to grow an existing market by a couple of percentage points.

Without making the brief too concrete, he helped the team establish a realistic set of goals. Without making it too broad, he left us space to interpret the concept for ourselves, to explore and to discover.

As the project progressed and new insights accumulated, it seemed advisable to adjust the initial plan by introducing additional constraints: a revised price point; a restriction that there be "no electric motors." Such midcourse adjustments are common and are a natural feature of a process that is healthy, flexible, and dynamic. The modifications to the original brief helped Ronn to specify the level of cost and complexity that was appropriate for his business.

Simultaneously, these continual refinements of the initial plan helped guide the project team toward the right balance of feasibility, viability, and desirability. Over the course of about twelve weeks, this well-crafted brief led to a staggering 350 product concepts, more than 60 prototypes, and 3 ideas that advanced to development. One of them—Mr. Clean Magic Reach, a multifunctional tool that met every one of the stated criteria—went into production eighteen months later.

The message here is that design thinking needs to be practiced on both sides of the table: by the design team, obviously, but by the client as well. I cannot count the number of clients who have marched in and said, "Give me the next iPod," but it's probably pretty close to the number of designers I've heard respond (under their breath), "Give me the next Steve Jobs." The difference between a design brief with just the right level of constraint and one that is overly vague or overly restrictive can be the difference between a team on fire with breakthrough ideas and one that delivers a tired reworking of existing ones.

## smart teams

The next ingredient is clearly the *project team*. Though it is possible to operate as an individual (the garages of Silicon Valley are still full of lone inventors aspiring to become the next Bill Hewlett or Dave Packard), the complexity of most of today's projects is fast relegating this type of practice to the margins. Even in the more traditional design fields of industrial and graphic design, not to say architecture, teams have been the norm for years. An automobile company has dozens of designers working on each new model. A new building may involve hundreds of architects. As design begins to tackle a wider range of problems—and to move upstream in the innovation process—the lone designer, sitting alone in a studio and meditating upon the relation between form and function, has yielded to the interdisciplinary team.

Although we will never, I hope, lose respect for the designer as inspired form giver, it is common now to see designers working with psychologists and ethnographers, engineers and scientists, marketing and business experts, writers and filmmakers. All of these disciplines, and many more, have long contributed to the development of new products and services, but today we are bringing them together within the same team, in the same space, and using the same processes. As MBAs learn to talk to MFAs and PhDs across their disciplinary divides (not to mention to the occasional CEO, CFO, and CTO), there will be increasing overlap in activities and responsibilities.

There is a popular saying around IDEO that "all of us are smarter than any of us," and this is the key to unlocking the creative power of any organization. We ask people not simply to offer expert advice on materials, behaviors, or software but to be active in each of the spaces of innovation: inspiration, ideation, and implementation. Staffing a project with people from diverse backgrounds and a multiplicity of disciplines takes some patience, however. It requires us to identify individuals who are confident enough of their expertise that they are willing to go beyond it.

To operate within an interdisciplinary environment, an individual needs to have strengths in two dimensions—the "T-shaped" person made famous by McKinsey & Company. On the vertical axis, every member of the team needs to possess a depth of skill that allows him or her to make tangible contributions to the outcome. This competence—whether in the computer lab, in the machine shop, or out in the field—is difficult to acquire but easy to spot. It may be necessary to sift through literally thousands of résumés to find those unique individuals, but it is worth the effort.

But that is not enough. Many designers who are skilled technicians, craftsmen, or researchers have struggled to survive in the messy environment required to solve today's complex problems. They may play a valuable role, but they are destined to live in the downstream world of design execution. Design thinkers, by contrast, cross the "T." They may be architects who have studied psychology, artists with MBAs, or engineers with marketing experience. A creative organization is constantly on the lookout for people with the capacity and—just as important— the disposition for collaboration across disciplines. In the end, this ability is what distinguishes the merely *multidisciplinary* team from a truly *interdisciplinary* one. In a multidisciplinary team each individual becomes an advocate for his or her own technical specialty and the project becomes a protracted negotiation among them, likely resulting in a gray compromise. In an interdisciplinary team there is collective ownership of ideas and everybody takes responsibility for them.

## teams of teams

Design thinking is the opposite of group thinking, but paradoxically, it takes place in groups. The usual effect of "groupthink," as William H. Whyte explained to the readers of *Fortune* back in 1952, is to suppress people's creativity. Design thinking, by contrast, seeks to liberate it. When a team of talented, optimistic, and collaborative design thinkers comes together, a chemical change occurs that can lead to unpredictable actions and reactions. To reach this point, however, we have learned that we must channel this energy productively, and one way to achieve this is to do away with one large team in favor of many small ones.

Though it is not uncommon to see large creative teams at work, it is nearly always in the implementation phase of the project; the inspiration phase, by contrast, requires a small, focused group whose job is to establish the overall framework. When Chief Designer Tom Matano presented the Miata concept to Mazda's leadership in August 1984, he was accompanied by two other designers, a product planner, and a couple of engineers. By the time the project neared completion, his team had grown to thirty or forty. The same can be said of any major architectural project, software project, or entertainment project. Look at the credits on your next movie rental, and check out the preproduction phase. There will invariably be a small team consisting of director, writer, producer, and production designer who have developed the basic concept. Only later do the "armies" arrive.

As long as the objective is simple and limited, this approach works. Faced with more complex problems, we may be tempted to increase the size of the core team early on, but more often than not this leads to a dramatic reduction in speed and efficiency as communications within the team begin to take up more time than the creative process itself. Are there alternatives? Is it possible to preserve the effectiveness of small teams while tackling more complex, system-level problems? It is increasingly clear that new technology—properly designed and wisely deployed—can help leverage the power of small teams.

The promise of electronic collaboration should not be to create dispersed but ever-bigger teams; this tendency merely compounds the political and bureaucratic problems we are trying to solve. Rather, our goal should be to create interdependent networks of small teams as has been done by the online innovation exchange Innocentive. Any company that has an R&D problem can post a challenge on Innocentive and it will be exposed to tens of thousands of scientists, engineers, and designers who can choose to submit solutions. The Internet, in other words, characterized by dispersed, decentralized, mutually reinforcing networks, is not so much the *means* as the *model* of the new forms of organization taking shape. Because it is open-sourced and open-ended, it allows the energy of many small teams to be brought to bear on the same problem.

Progressive companies are now grappling with a second, related problem. As the issues confronting us become more complex—intricate, multinational supply chains; rapid changes in technology platforms; the sudden appearance and disappearance of discrete consumer groups—the need to involve a number of specialists grows. This challenge is difficult enough when a group is physically in the same place, but it becomes far more challenging when critical input is required from partners dispersed around the globe.

Much effort has gone into the problem of remote collaboration. Videoconferencing, although invented in the 1960s, became widespread once digital telephony networks became technically feasible in the 1980s. Only recently has it begun to show signs of taking hold as an effective medium of remote collaboration. E-mail has done little to support collective teamwork. The Internet helps move information around but has done little to bring people together. Creative teams need to be able to share their thoughts not only verbally but visually and physically as well. I am not at my best writing memos. Instead, put me in a room where somebody is sketching on a whiteboard, a couple of others are writing notes on Post-its or sticking Polaroid photos on the wall, and somebody is sitting on the floor putting together a quick prototype. I haven't yet heard of a remote collaboration tool that can substitute for the give-and-take of sharing ideas in real time.

So far, efforts to innovate around the topic of remote groups have suffered from a lack of understanding about what motivates creative teams and supports group collaboration. Too much has been focused on mechanical tasks such as storing and sharing data or running a structured meeting and not enough on the far messier tasks of generating ideas and building a consensus around them. Recently, however, there have been promising signs of change. The emergence of social networking sites has shown that people are driven to connect, share, and "publish," even if there is no immediate reward to be gained. No economic model could have predicted the success of MySpace and Facebook. Technological initiatives such as the new "telepresence" systems being developed by Hewlett-Packard and Cisco Systems, will represent a quantum leap over the videoconferencing systems currently in use.

Numerous smaller-scale tools are already available. "Always on" video links (also called "wormholes") encourage spontaneous interactions among team members at different sites and increase a group's access to people with expertise located in another city, state, or continent. This capability is important because good ideas rarely come on schedule and may wither and die in the interludes between weekly meetings. Instant messaging, blogs, and wikis all allow teams to publish and share insights and ideas in new ways—with the advantage that an expensive IT support team is not necessary as long as someone on the team has a family member in junior high school. After all, none of these tools existed a decade ago (the Internet itself, as the technovisionary Kevin Kelly has remarked, is fewer than five thousand days old!). All are leading to new experiments in collaboration and hence to new insights into the interactions of teams. Anyone who is serious about design thinking across an organization will encourage them.

## cultures of innovation

Google has slides, pink flamingos, and full-size inflatable dinosaurs. Pixar has beach huts. IDEO will erupt into a pitched FingerBlaster war on the slightest provocation.

It's hard not to trip over the evidence of the creative cultures for which each of these companies is famous, but these emblems of innovation are just that—emblems. To be creative, a place does not have to be crazy, kooky, and located in northern California. What *is* a prerequisite is an environment—social but also spatial—in which people know they can experiment, take risks, and explore the full range of their faculties. It does little good to identify the brightest T-shaped people around, assemble them in interdisciplinary teams, and network them to other teams if they are forced to work in an environment that dooms their efforts from the start. The physical and psychological spaces of an organization work in tandem to define the effectiveness of the people within it.

A culture that believes that it is better to ask forgiveness *afterward* rather than permission *before*, that rewards people for success but gives them permission to fail, has removed one of the main obstacles to the formation of new ideas. If Gary Hamel is correct in arguing that the twenty-first century will favor adaptability and continuous innovation, it just makes sense that organizations whose "product" is creativity should foster environments that reflect and reinforce it. Relaxing the rules is not about letting people be silly so much as letting them be whole people—a step many companies seem reluctant to take. Indeed, the fragmentation of individual employees is often just a reflection of the fragmentation of the organization itself. I have observed many situations in which the supposedly "creative" designers are sequestered from the rest of the company. Although they may have a merry time off in their studios, this isolation quarantines them and undermines the creative efforts of the organization from opposite angles: the designers are cut off from other sources of knowledge and expertise, while everyone else is given the demoralizing message that theirs is the nine-to-five world of business attire and a sober business ethic. Would the U.S. auto industry have reacted faster to changes in the market if designers, marketers, and engineers had been sitting around the same table? Perhaps.

The concept of "serious play" has a long, rich history within American social science, but nobody understands it in more practical terms than Ivy Ross. As senior VP of design for girls' products at Mattel, Ross realized that Mattel had made it difficult for the various disciplines across the company to communicate and collaborate. To address this she created Platypus, the code name for a twelve-week experiment in which participants from across the organization were invited to relocate to an alternative space with the objective of creating new and out-of-the-box product ideas. "Other companies have skunk works," Ross told *Fast Company*. "We have a platypus. I looked up the definition, and it said, 'an uncommon mix of different species.'"

Indeed, the species at Mattel could hardly have been more different: people came from finance, marketing, engineering, and design. The only requirement was that they commit themselves full-time to Platypus for three months. Since many of them had never been involved in new product development before and few had any kind of creative training, the first two weeks of the session were spent in a "creativity boot camp." There they heard from a spectrum of experts about everything from child development to group psychology and were exposed to a range of new skills including improvised acting, brainstorming, and prototyping. During the remaining ten weeks they explored new directions for girls' play and came up with a series of innovative product concepts. By the end they were ready to pitch their ideas to management.

Although it was located literally in the shadow of the company's headquarters in El Segundo, California, Platypus created a space that challenged all of the corporate rules. Ross regularly brought new teams together and put them into an environment designed to let people experiment in ways they had never been able to in their normal jobs. As she predicted, many Platypus graduates went back to their respective departments determined to use the practices and ideas they had learned. They found, however, that the culture of efficiency to which they returned invariably made that difficult. More than a few became frustrated. Some ultimately left the company.

Clearly, it is not enough to inject selected people into a specialized environment designed for skunks, platypi, or other risk-taking creatures. They may indeed unleash their creative imaginations, but there must also be a plan for reentry into the organization. Claudia Kotchka understood this need when she created the Clay Street Project for Procter & Gamble—named for a loft in downtown Cincinnati where project teams can get away from the day-to-day distractions and think like designers. The theory of Clay Street is that a division—Hair Care or Pet Care, for example—funds and staffs each project, and teams that create particularly strong ideas are encouraged to shepherd them through execution and launch. This was the hothouse environment in which the dated Herbal Essences brand was transformed into a fresh, successful new range of products. The people who have experienced Clay Street return to their departments with new skills and new ideas that they can apply with the full permission of the company.

# how using real space helps the process

Although it can at times seem forbiddingly abstract, design thinking is *embodied* thinking—embodied in teams and projects, to be sure, but embodied in the physical spaces of innovation as well. In a culture of meetings and milestones, it can be difficult to support the exploratory and iterative processes that are at the heart of the creative process. Happily, there are tangible things we can do to ensure that facilities do what they are supposed to do: *facilitate!* IDEO allocates special "project rooms" that are reserved to a team for the duration of its work. In one room a group will be thinking about the future of the credit card; next to it a team is working on a device to prevent deep-vein thrombosis among hospital patients, and another planning a clean water distribution system for rural India for the Bill and Melinda Gates Foundation. The project spaces are large enough that the accumulated research materials, photos, storyboards, concepts, and prototypes can be out and available all of the time. The simultaneous visibility of these project materials helps us identify patterns and encourages creative synthesis to occur much more readily than when these resources are hidden away in file folders, notebooks, or PowerPoint decks. A well-curated project space, augmented by a project Web site or wiki to help keep team members in touch when they are out in the field, can significantly improve the productivity of a team by supporting better collaboration among its members and better communication with outside partners and clients.

So integral are these project spaces to our creative process that we have exported them, whenever possible, to our clients. Procter & Gamble has built the Gym in Cincinnati, an innovation lab that R&D teams use to turbocharge their projects and move more quickly to tangible prototypes. Steelcase has built its Learning Center in Grand Rapids, a corporate education facility that doubles as a design thinking space. On any given day the center's team rooms and project spaces might be claimed by employees taking classes on management techniques, customers learning about how the company's products can enhance collaboration, or senior leaders huddled together to discuss future strategy. These ideas have even made their way into the precincts of higher education. For the Stanford Center for Innovations in Learning, an IDEO team, working with the SCIL's educational research experts, developed several floors of adaptable, reconfigurable spaces. Because of the inherently tentative and experimental nature of design thinking, flexibility is a key element of its success. As Dilbert has shown, regulation-size spaces tend to produce regulation-size ideas.

There is an important lesson here about the challenges of shifting from a culture of hierarchy and efficiency to one of risk taking and exploration. Those who navigate this transition successfully are likely to become more deeply engaged, more highly motivated, and more wildly productive than they have ever been before. They will show up early and stay late because of the enormous satisfaction they get from giving form to new ideas and putting them out into the world. Once they have experienced this feeling, few people will be willing to give it up.

Over the course of their century-long history of creative problem solving, designers have acquired a set of tools to help them

move through what I have called the "three spaces of innovation": inspiration, ideation, and implementation. My argument is that these skills now need to be dispersed throughout
organizations. In particular, design thinking needs to move
"upstream," closer to the executive suites where strategic decisions are made. Design is now too important to be left to
designers.

It may be perplexing for those with hard-won design degrees to imagine a role for themselves beyond the studio,
just as managers may find it strange to be asked to think like
designers. But this should be seen as the inevitable result of
a field that has come of age. The problems that challenged
designers in the twentieth century—crafting a new object,
creating a new logo, putting a scary bit of technology into a
pleasing or at least innocuous box—are simply not the problems that will define the twenty-first. If we are to deal with
what Bruce Mau has called the "massive change" that seems
to be characteristic of our time, we all need to think like
designers.

Just as I am challenging companies to incorporate design
into their organizational DNA, however, I want to challenge
designers to continue the transformation of design practice itself. There will always be a place in our dizzying world for
the artist, the craftsman, and the lone inventor, but the seismic shifts taking place in every industry demand a new design
practice: collaborative but in a way that amplifies, rather than
subdues, the creative powers of individuals; focused but at the
same time flexible and responsive to unexpected opportunities;
focused not just on optimizing the social, the technical, and
the business components of a product but on bringing them

into a harmonious balance. The next generation of designers will need to be as comfortable in the boardroom as they are in the studio or the shop, and they will need to begin looking at every problem—from adult illiteracy to global warming—as a *design* problem.

# converting need into demand,
## or *putting people first*

Several years ago, during the research phase for a project on office telephone systems, we interviewed a travel agent who had developed a startlingly effective "workaround" for making conference calls. Rather than contend with her company's impossibly complicated phone system, she simply dialed each party on a separate telephone and arrayed the receivers around her desk—"Judy" in Minneapolis was on her left; "Marvin" in Tampa was on her right; and together the three of them figured out a complicated travel itinerary. The software engineers who labored over the interface would have probably resorted to the standard lament: "RTFM"—"Read the (ahem) Manual." For design thinkers, however, behaviors are never right or wrong, but they are always meaningful.

The job of the designer, to borrow a marvelous phrase from Peter Drucker, is "converting need into demand." On the face of it, this sounds simple: just figure out what people want and then give it to them. But if it's so easy, why don't we see more success stories like the iPod? The Prius? MTV and eBay? The answer, I'd suggest, is that we need to return human beings to the center of the story. We need to learn to put people first.

Much has been written about "human-centered design" and its importance to innovation. Since there are so few truly compelling stories, however, it's time to ask why it is so difficult to spot a need and design a response. The basic problem is that people are so ingenious at adapting to inconvenient situations that they are often not even aware that they are doing so: they sit on their seat belts, write their PINs on their hands, hang their jackets on doorknobs, and chain their bicycles to park benches. Henry Ford understood this when he remarked, "If I'd asked my customers what they wanted, they'd have said 'a faster horse.'" This is why traditional techniques such as focus groups and surveys, which in most cases simply ask people what they want, rarely yield important insights. The tools of conventional market research can be useful in pointing toward incremental improvements, but they will never lead to those rule-breaking, game-changing, paradigm-shifting breakthroughs that leave us scratching our heads and wondering why nobody ever thought of them before.

Our real goal, then, is not so much fulfilling manifest needs by creating a speedier printer or a more ergonomic keyboard; that's the job of designers. It is helping people to articulate the latent needs they may not even know they have, and this is the challenge of *design thinkers*. How should we approach it? What tools do we have that can lead us from modest incremental changes to the leaps of insight that will redraw the map? In this chapter I'd like to focus upon three mutually reinforcing elements of any successful design program. I'll call them *insight, observation, and empathy*.

## insight: learning from the lives of others

Insight is one of the key sources of design thinking, and it does not usually come from reams of quantitative data that measure exactly what we already have and tell us what we already know. A better starting point is to go out into the world and observe the actual experiences of commuters, skateboarders, and registered nurses as they improvise their way through their daily lives. The psychologist Jane Fulton Suri, one of the pioneers of human factors research, refers to the myriad "thoughtless acts" people perform throughout the day: the shopkeeper who uses a hammer as a doorstop; the office worker who sticks identifying labels onto the jungle of computer cables under his desk. Rarely will the everyday people who are the consumers of our products, the customers for our services, the occupants of our buildings, or the users of our digital interfaces be able to tell us what to do. Their actual behaviors, however, can provide us with invaluable clues about their range of unmet needs.

Design is a fundamentally creative endeavor, but I do not mean this in an arcane or romantic sense. In an analytical paradigm, we simply solve for the missing number (though anyone who struggled, as I did, through high school algebra knows how daunting this can be!). In a *design* paradigm, however, the solution is not locked away somewhere waiting to be discovered but lies in the creative work of the team. The creative process generates ideas and concepts that have not existed before. These are more likely to be triggered by observing the odd practices of an amateur carpenter or the incongruous detail in a mechanic's shop than by hiring expert consultants or asking "statistically average" people to respond to a survey or fill out a questionnaire. The insight phase that helps to launch a project is therefore every bit as critical as the engineering that comes later, and we must take it from wherever we can find it.

The evolution from *design* to *design thinking* is the story of the evolution from the creation of products to the analysis of the relationship between people and products, and from there to the relationship between people and people. Indeed, a striking development of recent years has been the migration of designers toward social and behavioral problems, such as adhering to a drug regimen or shifting from junk food to healthy snacking. When the Centers for Disease Control and Prevention approached IDEO with the challenge of addressing the epidemic of obesity among children and teens, we seized the opportunity to apply these qualitative research practices to a problem where we might have real social impact. In search of insight, a team of human factors experts called Jennifer Portnick at Feeling Good Fitness in San Francisco.

Jennifer had nurtured the dream of becoming a Jazzercise dance instructor but at a full-figured size 18 she ran up against the company's requirement that franchisees project "a fit appearance." She countered that "fit" and "large" are not incompatible and persisted through a legal challenge that won international attention and led Jazzercise to drop its weight-discriminatory policy. Portnick's story has been inspiring to countless people—of all sizes and both sexes— who have faced discrimination on account of acquired or inherited characteristics. It was inspiring to design thinkers, however, on different grounds. Because she flourished on the margins of the bell curve, she was in a position to help the design team frame the problem in a new and insightful way. To begin with the assumption that all fat people want to be thin, that weight is inversely proportional to happiness, or that large size implies lack of discipline is to prejudge the problem.

The single example of Jennifer Portnick gave the project team more insight into the problem of youth obesity than reams of statistics. And the easiest thing about the search for insight—in contrast to the search for hard data—is that it's everywhere and it's free.

## observation: watching what people don't do, listening to what they don't say

Walk into the offices of any of the world's leading design consultancies, and the first question is likely to be "Where is everybody?" Of course, many hours are spent in the model shop, in project rooms, and peering into computer monitors, but many more hours are spent out in the field with the people who will ultimately benefit from our work. Although grocery store shoppers, office workers, and schoolchildren are not the ones who will write us a check at the end of a project, they are our ultimate clients. The only way we can get to know them is to seek them out where they live, work, and play. Accordingly, almost every project we undertake involves an intensive period of observation. We watch what people do (and do not do) and listen to what they say (and do not say). This takes some practice.

There is nothing simple about determining whom to observe, what research techniques to employ, how to draw useful inferences from the information gathered, or when to begin the process of synthesis that begins to point us toward a solution. As any anthropologist will attest, observation relies on quality, not quantity. The decisions one makes can dramatically affect the results one gets. It makes sense for a company to familiarize itself with the buying habits of people who inhabit the center of its current market, for they are the ones who will verify that an idea is valid on a large scale—a fall outfit for Barbie, for instance, or next year's feature on last year's car. By concentrating solely on the bulge at the center of the bell curve, however, we are more likely to confirm what we already know than learn something new and surprising. For insights at that level we need to head for the edges, the places where we expect to find "extreme" users who live differently, think differently, and consume differently—a collector who owns 1,400 Barbies, for instance, or a professional car thief.

Hanging out with obsessives, compulsives, and other deviants can be unnerving, though it certainly makes life interesting. Fortunately, it's not always necessary to go quite to these extremes. A few years ago, when the Swiss company Zyliss engaged IDEO to design a new line of kitchen tools, the team started out by studying children and professional chefs—neither of whom were the intended market for these mainstream products. For that very reason, however, both groups yielded valuable insights. A seven-year-old girl struggling with a can opener highlighted issues of physical control that adults have learned to disguise. The shortcuts used by a restaurant chef yielded unexpected insights into cleaning because of the exceptional demands he placed on his kitchen tools. The exaggerated concerns of people at the margins led the team to abandon the orthodoxy of the "matched set" and to create a line of products united by a common design language but with the right handle for each tool. As a result, Zyliss whisks, spatulas, and pizza cutters continue to fly off the shelves.

## the behavioral turn

Although most people can train themselves to become sensitive, skilled observers, some firms have come to rely upon seasoned professionals who guide every stage of this process; indeed, a striking feature of design practice today is the number of highly trained social scientists who have opted for careers outside academia. A few economists entered the government after World War I and a trickle of sociologists ventured into the private sector in the wake of World War II, but they were always regarded by their former academic colleagues with misgivings. Today, however, some of the most imaginative research in the behavioral sciences is being sponsored by companies that take design thinking seriously.

At Intel's campus in Beaverton, Oregon, a high-powered team of researchers led by Maria Bezaitis uses observational tools refined in academic social science to study a range of issues that will affect the company's business not at the end of the current quarter but in ten years: the future of digital money; how teenage girls use technology to protect their privacy; patterns of street life in the emerging multinational metropolis; the burgeoning community of people who live in "extreme homes" such as RVs. The psychologists, anthropologists, and sociologists in Bezaitis's People and Practices Research Group have fanned out around the globe in search of insights into cultural transformations that may or may not remain local phenomena. Why is a Silicon Valley chip maker interested in sponsoring a bunch of renegade social scientists to study people and practices in eastern Europe or western Africa? Because today only about 10 percent of the world's population has access to networked communications technology. Intel knows that it will have to be ready when "the next 10 percent" comes online.

Other industry leaders are no less committed to the principle of extracting insights from observations and using them to inspire future product offerings. Nokia's worldwide research is supported by the innovative ethnographic techniques developed by Jan Chipchase, an anthropologist who conducts "exploratory human behavioral field research" from his home base in Tokyo. Chipchase and his group believe that they have glimpsed the future in phenomena ranging from the morning bicycle commute across Ho Chi Minh City to the items people carry in Helsinki, Seoul, and Rio de Janeiro to the sharing of cell phones in Kampala, Uganda. The vast range of observations Chipchase and his colleagues have collected, together with the insights culled from them, will inform Nokia's future product offerings over the next three to fifteen years. Such work is fundamentally different from trendspotting, coolhunting, and seasonal market research.

There are professional affinities between academic social scientists and those who work in industry—they hold the same degrees, read the same journals, and attend the same conferences—but there are also differences. Academics are typically motivated by a scientific objective, whereas researchers such as Bezaitis and Chipchase are more attuned to the long-term practical implications of their findings. The next stage along this continuum is represented by a new breed of ethnographer who works within the compressed time frame of a project. In contrast to the isolated theorizing of individual academics or the clustering of social scientists in the research units of Intel or Nokia, these people work best when they are integrated into cross-disciplinary project teams that may include designers, engineers, and marketers. Their shared experiences will become essential sources of idea generation throughout the life of the project.

I have had many opportunities to observe this model of ethnographic practice among my colleagues at IDEO. In a project for an NGO called The Community Builders, the largest nonprofit developer of low- and mixed-income public housing in the United States, we assembled a team consisting of an anthropologist, an architect, and a human factors specialist. Together they interviewed builders, planners, and municipal authorities, and local entrepreneurs and service providers, but did not stop there. The real insights happened when the team arranged to stay overnight with three families at different income levels and with different life trajectories who lived in Park Duvalle, a mixed-income community in Kentucky.

This approach became even more salient on a subsequent project in which the team was trying to develop a tool kit to help NGOs implement human-centered design to meet the needs of subsistence farmers in Africa and Asia. This time, together with their partners from International Development Enterprises, they arranged overnight stays in farming villages in Ethiopia and Vietnam. Over time they were able to build a level of trust among people who might have been justifiably wary of visiting anthropologists or aid officials arriving in shiny SUVs, and this led in turn to a climate of honesty, empathy, and mutual respect.

Although the behavioral science researchers at places such

as Intel, Nokia, and IDEO are trained professionals, there are times when it makes sense to "deputize" our clients and enlist them in the hard work of conducting observations themselves. We thought nothing of putting a pocket-size notebook into the hands of Alan G. Lafley, the CEO of Procter & Gamble, and sending him out shopping for records on Berkeley's colorful Telegraph Avenue. Lafley is famous for his impatience with CEOs who are content to peer down upon the world from the executive suite or from the smoked-glass windows of a corporate limousine and for his willingness to venture out into the places where his customers live, work, and shop. This perspective is surely the basis of his widely reported pronouncement that "mass marketing is dead."

On other occasions, it is our clients themselves who take the lead and provide cues as to where we might look for insight. In the course of a project on emergency room care, undertaken with the Institute for Healthcare Improvement and the Robert Wood Johnson Foundation, a member of the IHI group reported on his experience at the Indianapolis 500. A smoking racecar pulled into a pit stop where a precision team of trained professionals, with state-of-the-art tools at the ready, assessed the situation and performed all the necessary repairs within seconds. Change a few words around, and you have an accurate description of a hospital trauma center. Of course, we also looked at real emergency room environments and observed physicians and nurses at work, but observing "analogous" situations—a pit stop at the Indy 500, a neighborhood fire station, an elementary school playground during recess—will often jolt us out of the frame of reference that makes it so difficult to see the larger picture.

## empathy: standing in the shoes (or lying on the gurneys) of others

It's possible to spend days, weeks, or months conducting research of this sort, but at the end of it all we will have little more than stacks of field notes, videotapes, and photographs unless we can connect with the people we are observing at a fundamental level. We call this "empathy," and it is perhaps the most important distinction between academic thinking and design thinking. We are not trying to generate new knowledge, test a theory, or validate a scientific hypothesis—that's the work of our university colleagues and an indispensable part of our shared intellectual landscape. The mission of design thinking is to translate observations into insights and insights into products and services that will improve lives.

Empathy is the mental habit that moves us beyond thinking of people as laboratory rats or standard deviations. If we are to "borrow" the lives of other people to inspire new ideas, we need to begin by recognizing that their seemingly inexplicable behaviors represent different strategies for coping with the confusing, complex, and contradictory world in which they live. The computer mouse developed at Xerox PARC in the 1970s was an intricate technical apparatus invented by engineers and intended for engineers. To them it made perfect sense that it should be taken apart and cleaned at the end of the day. But when the fledgling Apple Computer asked us to help it create a computer "for the rest of us," we gained our first lesson in the value of empathy.

A designer, no less than an engineer or marketing executive, who simply generalizes from his own standards and expectations will limit the field of opportunity. A thirty-year-old man does not have the same life experiences as a sixty-year-old woman. An affluent Californian has little in common with a tenant farmer living on the outskirts of Nairobi. A talented, conscientious industrial designer, settling down at her desk after an invigorating ride on her mountain bike, may be ill prepared to design a simple kitchen gadget for her grandmother who is suffering from rheumatoid arthritis.

We build these bridges of insight through *empathy*, the effort to see the world through the eyes of others, understand the world through their experiences, and feel the world through their emotions. In 2000, Robert Porter, the president and CEO of the SSM DePaul Health Center in Saint Louis, approached IDEO with a vision. Porter had seen the episode of ABC's *Nightline* in which Ted Koppel had challenged us to redesign the American shopping cart *in one week* and wanted to discuss the implications of our process for a new wing of the hospital. But we had a vision too, and we saw an opportunity for a new and radical "codesign" process that would join designers and health care professionals in a common effort. We challenged ourselves by starting with what is perhaps the most demanding of all hospital environments: the emergency room.

Drawing upon his highly specialized expertise in the ethnographic study of technology and complex systems, Kristian Simsarian, one of the core team members, set out to capture the patient experience. What better way to do so than to check into the hospital and go through the emergency room experience, from admission to examination, as if he were a patient? Feigning a foot injury, Kristian placed himself into the shoes—and in fact, onto the gurney—of the average emergency room patient. He saw firsthand how disorienting the check-in process could be. He experienced the frustration of being asked to wait, without ever being told what he was waiting for or why. He endured the anxiety of being wheeled by an unidentified staffer down an anonymous corridor through a pair of intimidating double doors and into the glare and the din of the emergency room.

We have all had those kinds of first-person, first-time experiences—buying our first car, stepping out of the airport in a city we have never visited, evaluating assisted living facilities for an aging parent. In these situations we look at everything with a much higher level of acuity because nothing is familiar and we have not fallen into the routines that make daily life manageable. With a video camera tucked discreetly beneath his hospital gown, Kristian captured a patient's experience in a way that no surgeon, nurse, or ambulance driver could possibly have done.

When Kristian returned from his undercover mission, the team reviewed the unedited video and spotted numerous opportunities for improving the patient experience. But there was a larger discovery. As they sat through minute after tedious minute of acoustic ceiling tiles, look-alike hallways, and featureless waiting areas, it became increasingly evident that these details, not the efficiency of the staff or the quality of the facilities, were key to the new story they wanted to tell. The crushing tedium of the video thrust the design team into Kristian's—and, by extension, the patient's—experience of the opacity of the hospital process. It triggered in each of them the mix of boredom and anxiety that comes with being in a situation in which one feels lost, uninformed, and not in control.

The team realized that two competing narratives were in play: The hospital saw the "patient journey" in terms of insurance verification, medical prioritization, and bed allocation. The patient experienced it as a stressful situation made worse. From this set of observations the team concluded that the hospital needed to balance its legitimate concerns with medical and administrative tasks with an empathic concern for the human side of the equation. This insight became the basis of a far-reaching program of "codesign" in which IDEO's designers worked with DePaul's hospital staff to explore hundreds of opportunities to improve the patient experience.

Kristian's visit to the emergency room exposed a layered picture of a patient's experience. At the most obvious level, we learned about his physical environment: we can see what he sees and touch what he touches; we observe the emergency room as an intense, crowded place that provides patients with few cues as to what is going on; we feel the cramped spaces and the narrow hallways and note both the structured and improvised interactions that take place within them. We may infer that the emergency room facilities—not unreasonably, perhaps—are designed around the requirements of the professional staff rather than the comfort of the patient. Insights lead to new insights as seemingly insignificant physical details accumulate.

A second layer of understanding is less physical than cognitive. By experiencing the patient journey firsthand, the team gained important clues that might help it to translate insight into opportunity. How does a patient make sense out of the situation? How do new arrivals navigate the physical and social space? What are they likely to find confusing? These questions are essential to identifying what we call *latent* needs, needs that may be acute but that people may not be able to articulate. By achieving a state of empathy with anxious patients checking into an emergency room (or weary travelers checking into a Marriott hotel or frustrated passengers checking in at an Amtrak ticket counter), we can better imagine how the experience might be improved. Sometimes we use these insights to emphasize the new. At other times it makes sense to do just the opposite, to reference the ordinary and the familiar.

Cognitive understanding of the ordinary and the familiar was at work when Tim Mott and Larry Tesler, working on the original graphical user interface at Xerox PARC in the 1970s, proposed the metaphor of the desktop. This concept helped move the computer from a forbidding new technology of value only to scientists to a tool that could be applied to office and even household tasks. It was still in evidence three decades later, when the start-up Juniper Financial asked IDEO to help it think about whether banks still needed buildings, vaults, and tellers.

In approaching the uncharted territory of online banking, we began by trying to get a better understanding of how people thought about their money. This exercise proved to be challenging in the extreme since we can't watch the *cognitive* process of someone thinking about money in the way we can watch the *behavioral* process of someone paying a bill or withdrawing cash from an ATM. The team settled on the technique of asking selected participants to "draw their money"—not the credit cards in their wallets or the checkbooks in their purses but the way in which money played a part in their lives. One participant—we called her "The Pathfinder"—drew little Monopoly-style houses representing her family, her 401(k) retirement plan, and some rental properties, since her focus was on long-term security. Another participant—designated "The Onlooker"—drew a picture with a pile of money on one side and a pile of goods on the other. With disarming candor, she explained to the team, "I get money and I buy stuff." The Onlooker was completely focused on her day-to-day financial situation and did almost no planning for the future. Beginning from cognitive experiments like these, the team of researchers, strategists, and designers developed a subtle market analysis that helped Juniper refine its target market and build an effective service in the emerging world of online banking.

A third layer—beyond the functional and the cognitive—comes into play when we begin working with ideas that matter to people at an emotional level. Emotional understanding becomes essential here. What do the people in your target population feel? What touches them? What motivates them? Political parties and advertising agencies have been exploiting people's emotional vulnerabilities for ages, but "emotional understanding" can help companies turn their customers not into adversaries but into advocates.

The Palm Pilot was an indisputably clever invention, and it has, deservedly, won widespread acclaim. Jeff Hawkins, its creator, began with the insight that the competition for a small, mobile device was not the omnifunctional laptop computer but the simple paper diary that many of us still slip into and out of our shirt pockets or purses a hundred times a day. When he began to work on the Palm in the mid-1990s, Jeff decided to buck the conventional wisdom and create a product that did *less* than was technically possible. That his software engineers could have stuffed spreadsheet capabilities, colorful graphics, and a garage-door opener into the Palm didn't matter. Better to do a few things well, so long as they were the *right* things: a contact list, a calendar, and a to-do list. Period.

The first version of the Palm PDA was a hit among tech-savvy early adopters, but there was nothing about its chunky gray plastic form that fired the imaginations of the larger public. In search of this elusive quality, Jeff teamed up with Dennis Boyle at IDEO, and together they began to work on a redesign that would appeal not just at a *functional* but also at an *emotional* level. The interface was left largely unchanged, but the physical quality of the device—designers call it the "form factor"—was reimagined. First, it was to be thin enough that it would slide smoothly into a pocket or purse—if it didn't disappear, Dennis sent his team back to the drawing boards. Second, it was to have a feel that was sleek, elegant, and sophisticated. The team sought out an aluminum-stamping technique used by Japanese camera manufacturers and found a rechargeable power supply that even the battery suppliers doubted would work. The added development was worth the effort. The Palm V went on sale in 1999, and sales rocketed to more than 6 million. It opened up the market for the handheld PDA not because of a lower price point, added functionality, or technical innovation. The elegant Palm V did everything it promised to do, but its sophisticated look and professional feel appealed, at an emotional level, to a whole new set of consumers.

## beyond the individual

If we were interested only in understanding the individual consumer as a psychological monad, we could probably stop here;

we have learned to observe him in his natural habitat and gain insight from his behaviors; we have learned that we must empathize, not simply scrutinize with the cold detachment of statisticians. But even empathy for the individual, as it turns out, is not sufficient. To the extent that designers have one at all, their prevailing concept of "markets" remains the aggregate of many individuals. It rarely extends to how groups interact with one another. Design thinkers have upped the ante, beginning with the premise that the whole is greater than the sum of its parts.

With the growth of the Internet, it has become clear that we must extend our understanding to the social interactions of people within groups and to the interactions among groups themselves. Almost any Web-based service—from social networking sites to mobile phone offerings to the vast world of online gaming—requires an understanding of the dynamic interactions within and between larger groups. What are people trying to achieve as individuals? What group effects, such as "smart mobs" or "virtual economies," are taking shape? And how does membership in an online community affect the behavior of individuals once they return to the prosaic world of atoms, proteins, and bricks? It is hard to imagine creating anything today without trying to gain an understanding of group effects. Even a chair.

When Steelcase, the giant office furniture manufacturer, sits down with its customers to help them plan the right workplace environments, the designers use network analysis to understand who in their organization interacts with whom and which departments, functions, or even individuals should be colocated. Only then does it make sense to begin thinking about desks, storage units, and ergonomic chairs. We may use similar approaches when we are designing systems to facilitate knowledge sharing within and between offices. Simply asking people to recount how they spend their time or with whom they regularly communicate can result in skewed information. Even with the best of intentions, people's memories are faulty and their answers are likely to reflect what they think should be the unvarnished facts. Tools such as video ethnography (in which cameras record group behavior over time) and computer interaction analysis help gather more accurate data about the dynamic interactions among people and groups.

A second set of considerations is forcing us to rethink our notions of how to connect to consumers, and that is the pervasive fact of cultural differences—a theme that has moved from bad jokes about "political correctness" to the center of our concerns as we confront the realities of a media-saturated, globally interconnected society. Clearly, Kristian Simsarian's first-person observations of an emergency room would have yielded an entirely different set of insights if they had taken place in sub-Saharan Africa rather than suburban America.

This reality puts yet another dent in the idealized image of the designer as the source of professional expertise that can be taught in school, honed in professional practice, and exported universally to anyone in need of a better desk lamp or digital camera. Spending time to understand a culture can open up new innovation opportunities. This may help us to discover universal solutions that have relevance beyond our own culture, but they will always have their origins in empathy.

The movement from insight to observation to empathy leads us, finally, to the most intriguing question of them all: if cultures are so diverse and if the twentieth-century image of "the unruly mob" has given way to the twenty-first-century discovery of "the wisdom of crowds," how can we tap that collective intelligence to unleash the full power of design thinking? The designer must not be imagined as an intrepid anthropologist, venturing into an alien culture to observe the natives with the utmost objectivity. Instead we need to invent a new and radical form of collaboration that blurs the boundaries between creators and consumers. It's not about "us versus them" or even "us on behalf of them." For the design thinker, it has to be "us *with* them."

In the past, the consumer was viewed as the object of analysis or, worse, as the hapless target of predatory marketing strategies. Now we must migrate toward ever-deeper collaboration not just among members of a design team but between the team and the audience it is trying to reach. As Howard Rheingold has shown in his studies of "smart mobs" and Jeff Howe has demonstrated through "crowdsourcing" (more formally known as "distributed participatory design"), new technologies are suggesting promising ways of forging this link.

We are in the midst of a significant change in how we think about the role of consumers in the process of design and development. In the early years, companies would dream up new products and enlist armies of marketing experts and advertising professionals to sell them to people—often by exploiting their fears and vanities. Slowly this began to yield to a more nuanced approach that involved reaching out to people, observing their lives and experiences, and using those insights to inspire new ideas. Today, we are beginning to move beyond even this "ethnographic" model to approaches inspired and underpinned by new concepts and technologies.

My colleague Jane Fulton Suri has even begun to explore the next stage in the evolution of design as it migrates from designers creating *for* people to designers creating *with* people to people creating *by themselves* through the application of user-generated content and open-source innovation. The idea of "Everyman the Designer" is a compelling one, but the ability of consumers to generate breakthrough ideas on their own—as opposed to replicating existing ideas more efficiently and cheaply—is far from proven. Mozilla, with its Firefox Web browser, is one of the few companies to have been able to build a significant brand using an open-source approach.

These limitations do not mean that user-generated content is not interesting or that it may not become the Next Big Thing to roil out of the innovation cauldron. It has been argued that user-generated content is leading to far greater engagement and participation in the world of music than we ever saw during the top-down reign of mass media. Perhaps, but even the most zealous advocates of open-source design will admit that it has not produced its Mozart, John Lennon, or Miles Davis. Not yet, at any rate.

For the moment, the greatest opportunity lies in the middle space between the twentieth-century idea that companies created new products and customers passively consumed them and the futuristic vision in which consumers will design everything they need for themselves. What lies in the middle is an enhanced level of *collaboration* between creators and consumers, a blurring of the boundaries at the level of both companies and individuals. Individuals, rather than allowing themselves to be stereotyped as "consumers," "customers," or "users," can now think of themselves as active participants in the process of creation; organizations, by the same token, must become more comfortable with the erosion of the boundary between the proprietary and the public, between themselves and the people whose happiness, comfort, and welfare allow them to succeed.

We see evidence of innovative strategies meant to enhance the collaboration between creators and consumers everywhere. In an initiative funded by the European Union to look at ways in which digital technology might strengthen the fabric of society, Tony Dunne and Bill Gaver of the Royal College of Art in London developed a set of "cultural probes"—journal exercises, inexpensive video cameras—that enabled elderly villagers to document the patterns of their everyday lives. In industries more geared to the youth culture—video games, sports apparel—it is now quite common for developers to work with tech-savvy youths at every stage of the development process from concept development to testing. Sweat Equity Enterprises in New York (the term refers to contributing time and effort to a project as opposed to "financial equity," or money) works with companies as diverse as Nike, Nissan, and Radio Shack to codevelop new products with inner-city high school kids. The sponsoring companies capture cutting-edge insights "from the street" (a somewhat more reliable source of creativity than the executive suite) while at the same time making a lasting investment in education and opportunity for underserved urban youth.

One of the techniques we have developed at IDEO to keep the consumer-designer involved in the creation, evaluation, and development of ideas is the "unfocus group," where we bring an array of consumers and experts together in a workshop format to explore new concepts around a particular topic. Whereas traditional focus groups assemble a random group of "average" people who are observed, literally or figuratively, from behind a one-way mirror, the unfocus group identifies unique individuals and invites them to participate in an active, collaborative design exercise.

On one memorable occasion—we were looking at new concepts for women's shoes—we invited in a color consultant, a spiritual guide who led barefoot initiates across hot coals, a young mother who was curiously passionate about her thigh-high leather boots, and a female limo driver whose full livery was accented by a pair of outrageously sexy stiletto heels. Needless to say, this group proved to be extremely articulate about the emotional connections among shoes, feet, and the human condition. By the time we released them back into the San Francisco demimonde they had inspired an exciting portfolio of ideas. Though drawers in the heels to hide secret items and raised patterns that targeted key acupressure points did not survive, the insights on which they were based prodded us to think about what people *really* desire from shoes.


One autumn day in 1940 the industrial designer Raymond Loewy was visited in his office by George Washington Hill, the president of the American Tobacco Company and one of the more colorful personalities in American business history. Hill offered Loewy $50,000 if he could improve upon the Lucky Strike package—a wager Loewy readily accepted—and, as he was leaving, turned to Loewy and asked when it would be ready. "Oh, I don't know, some nice spring morning I will feel like designing the Lucky package and you'll have it in a matter of hours. I'll call you then."

Today we no longer feel that we must sit patiently and wait for some outrageous insight to strike us. Inspiration always involves an element of chance, but, as Louis Pasteur observed in a famous lecture of 1854, "Chance only favors the prepared mind." Certain themes and variations—techniques of observation, principles of empathy, and efforts to move beyond the individual—can all be thought of as ways of preparing the mind of the design thinker to find insight: from the seemingly commonplace as well as the bizarre, from the rituals of everyday life but also the exceptional interruptions to those rituals, and from the average to the extreme. That insight cannot yet be codified, quantified, or even defined—not yet, at any rate—makes it the most difficult but also the most exciting part of the design process. There is no algorithm that can tell us where it will come from and when it will hit.

# a mental matrix,
## or *"these people have no process!"*

One way to help design thinking diffuse throughout an organization is for designers to make their clients part of the experience. We do this not just to give them the thrill of peering behind the wizard's curtain but because we find that we invariably get much better results when the client is on board and actively participating. But be forewarned: it can be messy! Imagine an avid theatergoer who is invited backstage to witness the chaos that lies behind even the most flawless performance—last-minute costume repairs, two-by-fours lying about everywhere, Hamlet standing outside the stage door having a cigarette while Ophelia chatters into her cell phone . . . or, as one client was heard to lament in a frantic call back to her office, "These people have no process!"

A few weeks later she had become a convert, promoting design thinking within her own company—a stolid, respectable organization renowned for its structure, discipline, and *process*. But as with all epiphanies, that's where the hard work begins. It is one thing to witness the power of design and even to participate in it, quite another to absorb it into one's thinking and patiently build it into the structure of an organization. Those of us who have spent long years at design school still find it hard to shake off dearly held assumptions about how to get things done. People from more methodical backgrounds may fear that the risks are too high and the margin of error is perilously slim.

What's the best way to orient first-time visitors to this new and unfamiliar terrain? Though there is no real substitute for actually doing it, I can impart a fair sense of the experience of design thinking—some navigational landmarks, perhaps, if not a complete road map.

In chapter 1, I introduced the idea that a design team should expect to move through three overlapping spaces over the course of a project: an *inspiration* space, in which insights are gathered from every possible source; an *ideation* space, in which those insights are translated into ideas; and an *implementation* space, in which the best ideas are developed into a concrete, fully conceived plan of action. Again, these are overlapping "spaces" rather than sequential stages of a lockstep methodology. Insights rarely arrive on schedule, and opportunities must be seized at whatever inconvenient time they present themselves.

Every design process cycles through foggy periods of seemingly unstructured experimentation and bursts of intense clarity, periods of grappling with the Big Idea and long stretches during which all attention focuses on the details. Each of these phases is different, and it's important—if only for the morale of the team—to recognize that each *feels* different and calls for different strategies.

One of our more jaded designers even devised a project mood chart that pretty accurately predicts how the team will feel at different phases of the project:

When a fresh team ventures out into the field to collect information, it is full of optimism. The process of synthesis—the

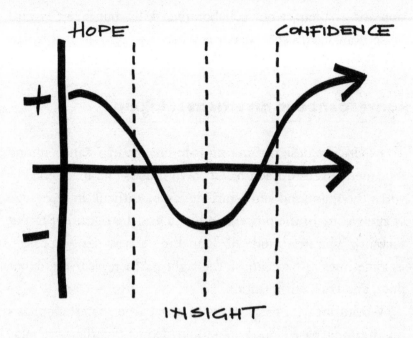

ordering of data and the search for patterns—can be frustrating as important decisions seem to ride on the most insubstantial of hunches. But then things begin to pick up. The ideation process becomes more tangible, and new concepts begin to take shape. The process peaks when the team begins to produce prototypes. Even if they don't look so good, don't work properly, or have too many features or too few, they are visible, tangible signs of progress. Eventually, once the right idea has been agreed upon, the project team settles down to a state of pragmatic optimism punctuated by moments of extreme panic. The scary bits never completely go away, but the experienced design thinker knows what to expect and is not undone by the occasional emotional slump. Design thinking is rarely a graceful leap from height to height; it tests our emotional constitution and challenges our collaborative skills, but it can reward perseverance with spectacular results.

## convergent and divergent thinking

To experience design thinking is to engage in a dance among four mental states. Each has its own moods and manners, but when the music suddenly starts it can be difficult to recognize where we are in the process and which is the right foot to put forward. The best guide, in launching a new design project, is sometimes just to choose the right partner, clear the dance floor, and trust our intuition.

Woven into the very fabric of our culture is an emphasis on thinking based upon logic and deduction; the psychologist Richard Nisbett, who has studied approaches to problem solving in Western and Eastern cultures, has gone so far as to suggest that there is a "geography of thought." Whether the problem lies in the domain of physics, economics, or history, Westerners are taught to take a series of inputs, *analyze* them, and then *converge upon* a single answer. At times we may find that the best—as opposed to the right—answer will have to do or that we may have to choose among equally compelling alternatives. Just think about the last time you and five friends had to agree on where to go out for dinner. Group thinking tends to converge toward a single outcome.

Convergent thinking is a practical way of deciding among existing alternatives. What convergent thinking is *not* so good at, however, is probing the future and creating new possibili-

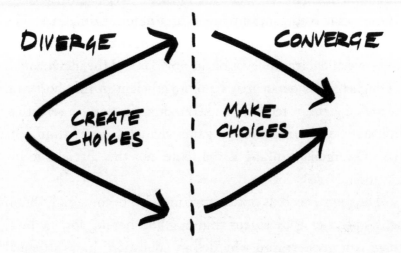

ties. Think of a funnel, where the flared opening represents a broad set of initial possibilities and the small spout represents the narrowly convergent solution. This is clearly the most efficient way to fill up a test tube or drive toward a set of fine-grained solutions.

If the convergent phase of problem solving is what drives us toward solutions, the objective of divergent thinking is to multiply options to create choices. These might be different insights into consumer behavior, alternative visions of new product offerings, or choices among alternative ways of creating interactive experiences. By testing competing ideas against one another, there is an increased likelihood that the outcome will be bolder, more creatively disruptive, and more compelling. Linus Pauling said it best: "To have a good idea, you must first have lots of ideas"—and he won *two* Nobel Prizes.

But we also need to be realistic. More choices means more complexity, which can make life difficult—especially for those whose job it is to control budgets and monitor timelines. The natural tendency of most companies is to constrain problems and restrict choices in favor of the obvious and the incremental. Though this tendency may be more efficient in the short run, in the long run it tends to make an organization conservative, inflexible, and vulnerable to game-changing ideas from outside. Divergent thinking is the route, not the obstacle, to innovation.

The point, then, is not that we must all become right-brain artists practicing divergent thinking and hoping for the best; there is a good reason why design education draws in equal measure upon art and engineering. The process of the design thinker, rather, looks like a rhythmic exchange between the divergent and convergent phases, with each subsequent iteration less broad and more detailed than the previous ones. In the divergent phase, new options emerge. In the convergent phase it is just the reverse: now it's time to *eliminate options* and *make choices*. It can be painful to let a once-promising idea fall away, and this is where the diplomatic skills of project leaders are often tested. William Faulkner, when asked what he found to be the most difficult part of writing, answered, "Killing off your little darlings."

## analysis and synthesis

Designers love to complain about "feature creep," the proliferation of unnecessary functions that add expense and complexity to otherwise straightforward products (RCA's original TV remote control device in 1958 had exactly one button; mine has forty-four). Design thinkers, for their part, need to be wary of what might be called "category creep." Nevertheless, I need to bring two additional terms into the discussion: *analysis* and *synthesis*, which are the natural complements to divergent and convergent thinking.

Without analytical forms of thinking we could not run large corporations or manage household budgets. Designers, too, whether they are looking at signage for a sports stadium or alternatives to carcinogenic PVCs, use analytical tools to break apart complex problems to understand them better. The creative process, however, relies on synthesis, the collective act of putting the pieces together to create whole ideas. Once the data have been gathered, it is necessary to sift through it all and identify meaningful patterns. Analysis and synthesis are equally important, and each plays an essential role in the process of creating options and making choices.

Designers carry out research in many ways: collecting ethnographic data in the field; conducting interviews; reviewing patents, manufacturing processes, vendors, and subcontractors. They can be found jotting notes, taking pictures, shooting videos, recording conversations, and sitting on airplanes. They are, hopefully, looking at the competition. Fact collecting and data gathering lead to an accumulation of information that can be staggering. But then what? At some point the team must settle down and in an intense period of synthesis—sometimes over the course of a few hours, sometimes over a week or more—begin to organize, interpret, and weave these many strands of data into a coherent story.

Synthesis, the act of extracting meaningful patterns from masses of raw information, is a fundamentally creative act; the data are just that—data—and the facts *never* speak for themselves. Sometimes the data are highly technical—if the task is a sophisticated piece of medical equipment, for instance; in other cases they may be purely behavioral, for example, if the problem is to encourage people to switch to energy-saving compact fluorescent bulbs. In every case we may think of the designer as a master storyteller whose skill is measured by his or her ability to craft a compelling, consistent, and believable narrative. It's no accident that writers and journalists now often work alongside mechanical engineers and cultural anthropologists in design teams.

Once the "raw material" has been synthesized into a coherent, inspiring narrative, a higher-level synthesis kicks in. It is far from unusual for a project brief to contain seemingly conflicting goals—low cost and high quality, to use an obvious example, or an accelerated time frame together with an interest in an unproven technology. There may be a tendency, under such circumstances, to simplify the process and reduce it to a set of specifications or a list of features. To do so is almost invariably to compromise the integrity of the product on the altar of convenience.

These are the seeds of design thinking—a continuous movement between divergent and convergent processes, on the one hand, and between the analytical and synthetic, on the other. But that is by no means the end of the story. As any gardener will attest, the hardiest seeds, cast into rocky or barren soil, will wither. The ground needs to be prepared. Attention must be shifted upward, from teams and individuals to companies. We might think of this as moving from the organization of design to the design of organizations.

## an attitude of experimentation

The master choreographers of the dance between divergent and convergent thinking, on the one hand, and detailed analysis and synthetic judgment, on the other, were Charles and Ray Eames, the most creative design partnership that America has produced. From their legendary office at 901 Washington Boulevard in Venice, California, the Eameses and their associates conducted a series of design experiments that stretched across four decades and covered every imaginable medium: the molded plywood chairs that became synonymous with American modernism; their famous Case Study House No. 8 in Pacific Palisades; the museum exhibitions they built, and the educational films they produced. Not always visible in the finished projects, however, is the methodical experimentation that lay behind them. The lesson? A creative team must be given the time, the space, and the budget to make mistakes.

Individuals, teams, and organizations that have mastered the mental matrix of design thinking share a basic attitude of experimentation. They are open to new possibilities, alert to new directions, and always willing to propose new solutions. Back in the 1960s, during the formative years of Silicon Valley, Chuck House, then an ambitious young engineer at Hewlett-Packard, came within a hair's breadth of losing his job. Following a hunch, he ignored an explicit corporate directive and set up an under-the-radar skunkworks to develop a large-screen CRT.

The illicit project went on to become the first commercially successful computer graphics display, used for the space video transmission of Neil Armstrong's foot-on-the-moon broadcast, Dr. Michael DeBakey's first artificial heart transplant monitor, and countless other applications. Chuck ended up as corporate engineering director for HP, with an office next door to David Packard himself, who had personally issued the prohibition against further research, and a "Medal of Defiance" hanging on his wall. Things have changed. He now runs Media X at Stanford University, a collaboration of industry and academia that brings together interactive technology researchers with companies committed to technical advancement and innovation. Today companies like Google and 3M are renowned for encouraging scientists and engineers to spend up to 20 percent of their time on personal experiments.

A tolerance for risk taking has as much to do with the culture of an organization as with its business strategy. Some would argue that a climate of open-ended exploration encourages a profligate waste of resources: Chairman Mao Zedong's policy during the Great Leap Forward, "Let a hundred flowers bloom," ended in complete disaster. But in contrast to the hermetically sealed environment of revolutionary China, the globalized economy today really is experiencing a "great leap forward." In an organization that encourages experimentation, there will be projects destined to go nowhere and still others that the keepers of institutional memory prefer not to talk about (remember the Apple Newton?). But to view such initiatives as "wasteful," "inefficient," or "redundant" may be a symptom of a culture focused on efficiency over innovation and a company at risk of collapsing into a downward spiral of incrementalism.

It's no accident that designers in recent years have been following the emerging science of biomimicry—the idea that nature, with its 4.5 billion–year learning curve, may have something to teach us about things such as nontoxic adhesives, minimal structures, efficient thermal insulation, or aerodynamic streamlining. The bewildering variety at work in a healthy ecosystem is nothing but an exercise in sustained experimentation—try something new, and see what sticks. It may well be that we need to begin mimicking nature not just at the molecular level but at the systemic level of companies and organizations. An excess of experimental zeal would be risky—companies do not enjoy the luxurious time frame of biological systems and their leaders would be remiss if they chose not to exercise what might be called—with apologies to Darwin—"intelligent design." What is called for is a judicious blend of bottom-up experimentation and guidance from above.

The rules for this approach are as simple to state as they are challenging to apply:

1. The best ideas emerge when the whole organizational ecosystem—not just its designers and engineers and certainly not just management—has room to experiment.

2. Those most exposed to changing externalities (new technology, shifting consumer base, strategic threats or opportunities) are the ones best placed to respond and most motivated to do so.

3. Ideas should not be favored based on who creates them. (Repeat aloud.)

4. Ideas that create a buzz should be favored. Indeed,

ideas should gain a vocal following, however small, before being given organizational support.

5.  The "gardening" skills of senior leadership should be used to tend, prune, and harvest ideas. MBAs call this "risk tolerance." I call it the top-down bit.

6.  An overarching purpose should be articulated so that the organization has a sense of direction and innovators don't feel the need for constant supervision.

These rules apply to almost every field of innovation. Together they ensure that the seeds of individual creativity take root—even in the aisles of a grocery store.

John Mackey, the CEO of Whole Foods Market, has applied this idea of bottom-up experimentation to his business since its founding, in 1980. Now the world's largest retailer of natural and organic foods, Whole Foods organizes each store's employees into small teams and encourages them to experiment with better ways to serve Whole Foods customers. These might include different display ideas or products selected to meet local customers' needs. Each store may have its own unique regional and even neighborhood identity. Managers are encouraged to share the best ideas so that they propagate outward across the company rather than remaining localized. None of this may sound all that revolutionary, but what Mackey has done since the earliest days of the company—he started with a single grocery store in Austin, Texas, and a total workforce of nineteen— is to make sure that every employee understands, appreciates, and has the ability to contribute to the overall vision of the company. These ideas act as navigational beacons for the localized innovations taking place throughout the organization.

As with each of the stories I've told, there is a moral to be drawn from this one: don't let the results of bottom-up experimentation dissipate into unstructured ideas and unresolved plans. Some companies provide suggestion boxes intended to harvest the bottom-up creativity of the organization. They tend to fail, leaving management to wonder why ungrateful employees pour coffee into them if they are hanging on the wall or flame them if they are online. At best they tend to yield small and incremental ideas. More often they go nowhere because there is no obvious mechanism for acting upon suggestions. What is needed is a serious commitment from the top of the corporate pyramid, and it will be repaid by better ideas from the base. Any promising experiment should have a chance to gain organizational support in the form of a project sustained by appropriate resources and driven by definable goals.

There is a simple test for this, though I have to admit that it has taken some getting used to: when I receive a cautiously worded memo asking for permission to try something, I find myself becoming equally cautious. But when I am ambushed in the parking lot by a group of hyperactive people falling all over one another to tell me about the unbelievably cool project they are working on, their energy infects me and my antennae go way, way up. Some of these projects will go wrong. Energy will be wasted (whatever that means) and money will be lost (we know exactly what that means). But even in these cases there is an old adage that remains worth pondering: in the words of my countryman Alexander Pope (back in the days when design thinkers did their best thinking in Latin), *"Errare humanum est, perdonare divinum"*—"To err is human, to forgive divine."

## a culture of optimism

The obvious counterpart to an attitude of experimentation is a climate of optimism. Sometimes the state of the world makes this difficult to sustain, but the fact remains that curiosity does not thrive in organizations that have grown cynical. Ideas are smothered before they have a chance to come to life. People willing to take risks are driven out. Up-and-coming leaders steer clear of projects with uncertain outcomes out of fear that participation might damage their chances for advancement. Project teams are nervous, suspicious, and prone to second-guessing what management "really" wants. Even when leadership wants to promote disruptive innovation and open-ended experimentation, it will find that no one is willing to step forward without permission—which usually means defeat before the start.

Without optimism—the unshakable belief that things could be better than they are—the will to experiment will be continually frustrated until it withers. Positive encouragement does not require the pretense that all ideas are created equal. It remains the responsibility of leadership to make discerning judgments, which will inspire confidence if people feel that their ideas have been given a fair hearing.

To harvest the power of design thinking, individuals, teams, and whole organizations have to cultivate optimism. People have to believe that it is within their power (or at least the power of their team) to create new ideas, that will serve unmet needs, and that will have a positive impact. When Steve Jobs returned to Apple in the summer of 1997 after being dismissed by his own board, he found a demoralized company that had spread its resources across no fewer than fifteen product platforms. Those teams were, in effect, competing with one another for survival. With all the boldness for which he is known, Jobs slashed the company's offerings from fifteen to four: a desktop and a laptop for professionals and a desktop and a laptop "for the rest of us." Every employee understood that the project he or she was working on represented fully one-quarter of Apple's business and there was no possibility that it would be killed by an accountant scrutinizing the balance sheets. Optimism soared, morale turned 180 degrees, and the rest, as the saying goes, is history. Optimism requires confidence, and confidence is built on trust. And trust, as we know, flows in both directions.

To find out whether a company is optimistic, experimental, and attuned to risk, people should simply use their senses: look for a colorful landscape of messy disorder rather than a suburban grid of tidy beige cubicles. Listen for bursts of raucous laughter rather than the constant drone of subdued conversation. Because IDEO does a great deal of work in the food and beverage industry, employs food scientists, and maintains an industrial kitchen, I can often literally *smell* excitement in the air. In general, try to be alert to the nodes where it all comes together, because that is where new ideas originate. I love to slip downstairs and observe members of a team at work building prototypes out of Legos or enacting an improvisational skit to explore a new service interaction. Above all, I love to be allowed to sit in on a brainstorm.

## brainstorming

Business school professors are fond of writing learned articles about the value of brainstorming. I encourage them to continue to do so (after all, some of my best friends are business school professors, and it keeps them busy and out of my way). Some surveys claim that motivated individuals can generate more ideas in the equivalent time working on their own. Other case studies demonstrate that brainstorming is as essential to creativity as exercise is to a healthy heart. As is so often the case, there is truth on both sides.

The skeptics certainly have a case: a well-intentioned manager who assembles a group of individuals who don't know one another, who are skeptical, and who lack confidence and gives them a tough problem to brainstorm is likely to get fewer viable ideas than if each of them had been sent away to think about the problem individually. Brainstorming, ironically, is a structured way of breaking out of structure. It takes practice.

As with cricket or football (or their American equivalents), there are rules for brainstorming. The rules lay out the playing field within which a team of players can perform at high levels. Without rules there is no framework for a group to collaborate within, and a brainstorming session is more likely to degenerate into either an orderly meeting or an unproductive free-for-all with a lot of talking and not much listening. Every organization has its own variations on the rules of brainstorming (just as every family seems to have its own version of Scrabble or Monopoly). At IDEO we have dedicated rooms for our brainstorming sessions, and the rules are literally written on the walls: Defer judgment. Encourage wild ideas. Stay focused on the topic. The most important of them, I would argue, is "Build on the ideas of others." It's right up there with "Thou shalt not kill" and "Honor thy father and thy mother," as it ensures that every participant is invested in the last idea put forward and has the chance to move it along.

Not long ago we were working on a kids' product for Nike. Although we have plenty of skilled toy designers on our staff, sometimes it makes sense to hire expert consultants to help us out. So we waited until their Saturday-morning cartoons were over and invited a group of eight-to-ten-year-olds to come in to our Palo Alto studios. After warming them up with orange juice and French toast, we split the boys and girls into two different rooms, gave them some instructions, and let them have at it for about an hour. When we gathered the results, the difference between the two groups was striking. The girls had come up with more than two hundred ideas whereas the boys had barely managed fifty. Boys, at this age, find it more difficult to focus and to listen—attributes essential to genuine collaboration. The girls were just the opposite. Fortunately, it's not my task to decide whether this disparity is the result of genetic inheritance, cultural norms, or birth order, but I can say that what we saw in these side-by-side brainstorms was real evidence of the power of building on the ideas of others. The boys, so eager to get their own ideas out there, were barely conscious of the ideas coming from their fellow brainstormers; the girls, without prompting, conducted a spirited but nonetheless *serial* conversation in which each idea related to the one that had come before and became a springboard to the one that came next. They were sparking off one another and getting better ideas as a result.

Brainstorming is not necessarily the ultimate technique for idea generation, and it cannot be built into the structure of every organization. But it does prove its worth when the goal is to open up a broad spectrum of ideas. Other approaches are important for *making* choices, but nothing beats a good brainstorming session for *creating* them.

# visual thinking

Design professionals spend years learning how to draw. Drawing practice is not so much in order to illustrate ideas, which can now be done with cheap software. Instead, designers learn to draw so that they can *express* their ideas. Words and numbers are fine, but only drawing can simultaneously reveal both the functional characteristics of an idea and its emotional content. To draw an idea accurately, decisions have to be made that can be avoided by even the most precise language; aesthetic issues have to be addressed that cannot be resolved by the most elegant mathematical calculation. Whether the task at hand is a hair dryer, a weekend retreat in the country, or an annual report, drawing forces decisions.

Visual thinking takes many forms. We should not suppose that it is restricted to objective illustration. In fact, it is not even necessary to possess drawing skills. In November 1972, relaxing in a late-night deli in Honolulu at the end of a long day of conference proceedings, a couple of biochemists took out a cocktail napkin and shared some crude drawings of bacteria having sex. A few years later Stanley Cohen was on a plane to Stockholm to collect his Nobel Prize and Herbert Boyer was pulling his red Ferrari into the parking lot of Genentech.

All children draw. Somewhere in the course of becoming logical, verbally oriented adults, they unlearn this elemental skill. Experts in creative problem solving such as Bob McKim, founder of Stanford's product design program, or the United Kingdom's prolific Edward de Bono, devoted much of their creative energy to mind maps, two-by-two matrices, and other visual frameworks that help explore and describe ideas in valuable ways.

When I use drawing to express an idea, I get different results than if I try to express it with words, and I usually get to them more quickly. I have to have a whiteboard or sketch pad nearby whenever I am discussing ideas with colleagues. I get stuck unless I can work it out visually. Leonardo da Vinci's sketchbooks are justly famous (no less a collector than Bill Gates snatched up the Hammer Codex when it came up for auction in 1994), but Leonardo didn't just use them to work out his own ideas. Often he simply stopped in the street to capture something he needed to figure out: a tangle of weeds; the curl of a cat sleeping in the sun; an eddy of water swirling in a gutter. Moreover, scholars poring over his mechanical drawings have punctured the myth that every sketch depicts his own inventions. Like any accomplished design thinker, Leonardo da Vinci used his drawing skills to build on the ideas of others.

## to post, or not to Post-it

Most people, by now, know the story of the humble Post-it note: Dr. Spencer Silver, a scientist working at 3M back in the 1960s, happened upon an adhesive with some curious properties. His employer, quite reasonably, did not see the utility of "inherently tacky elastomeric copolymer microspheres," aka glue that does not stick, and gave him little encouragement. It was not until one of his colleagues, Art Fry, began to use the adhesive to keep his bookmarks from falling out of his church hymnal that a plausible use was found for the little yellow notes. It is now a billion-dollar product and one of 3M's most valuable assets.

The Post-it note stands as an object lesson in how organiza-

tional timidity threatens to kill off a great idea. But those ubiq-
uitous little stickies have proven themselves to be an important
tool of innovation in and of themselves. Festooned on the walls
of project spaces, they have helped untold numbers of design
thinkers first to capture their wide-ranging insights and then to
order them into meaningful patterns. The Post-it note, in all its
pastel glory, embodies the movement from the divergent phase
that is the source of our inspiration to the convergent phase that
is the road map to our solutions.

The techniques of the design thinker that I have been
describing—brainstorming, visual thinking—contribute to the
*divergent* process of *creating* choices. But accumulating options
is merely an exercise if we do not move on to the *convergent*
phase of *making* choices. Doing so is critical if a project is to
move from a rousing exercise in creative idea generation toward a resolution. Just for that reason, however, it can be one
of the most difficult tasks that a design team faces. Given the
opportunity, every design team will diverge endlessly. There
is always a more interesting idea just around the corner, and
until the budget runs out they will happily turn one corner after
another. It is here that one of the simplest tools available for
convergence comes into play: the Post-it note.

Once everyone is gathered together for a project review, there
needs to be a process for selecting the ideas that are strongest
and hold the greatest promise. Storyboards help—panels that
illustrate, almost like comic strips, the sequence of events a user
might experience in checking into a hotel, opening a bank account, or using a newly purchased electronic device. Sometimes
it helps to create alternate scenarios. But sooner or later some
level of consensus is called for, and it rarely comes about by

debate or executive fiat. What is needed is some kind of tool to extract the intuition of the group, and this is where a generous supply of Post-it notes cannot be beat. At IDEO we use them to submit ideas to the "butterfly test."

Invented by Bill Moggridge, design thinker extraordinaire and one of the pioneers of Silicon Valley design, the butterfly test is a thoroughly unscientific but amazingly effective process for extracting a few key insights from a mass of data. Let's imagine that by the end of a deep research phase, numerous brainstorming sessions, and endless prototypes, an entire wall of the project room has been covered with promising ideas. Each participant is then given a small number of small Post-it "ballots" to attach to the ideas they think should move forward. Members of the team flutter about the room inspecting the tableau of ideas, and before long it is clear which ones have attracted the most "butterflies." Of course, all kinds of issues come into play, including politics and personalities, but that is what reaching consensus is all about. Give and take. Compromise and creative combination. All these and more play a part in reaching the end result. The process is not about democracy, it is about maximizing the capacities of teams to converge on the best solutions. It's chaotic, but it works surprisingly well and can be adapted to the peculiarities of many organizations.

I don't mean this to be an advertisement for 3M. The Post-it note, which encourages people to capture a quick thought, reposition it, or reject it, is just one of many tools available to deal with one insistent fact common to every design project: deadlines. Though we all have deadlines all of the time, in the divergent and exploratory phase of design thinking, deadlines take on an extra level of importance. They refer to the process and not the people. The deadline is the fixed point on the horizon where everything stops and the final evaluation begins. These points may seem arbitrary and unwelcome, but an experienced project leader knows how to use them to turn options into decisions. It's unwise to have a deadline every day, at least in the earlier phases of a project. Nor does it work to stretch it out for six months. It takes judgment to determine when a team will reach a point where management input, reflection, redirection, and selection are most likely to be valuable.

I have not yet met a client who says, "Take all the time you need." All project work is bound by limits: limits of technology, limits of skill, limits of knowledge. But the calendar is probably the most insistent limit of them all because it brings us back to the bottom line. As Ben Franklin, America's first and most adventurous real design thinker, pointed out in a letter to a young tradesman, "Time is money."

I have saved for last the single most powerful tool of design thinking. This is not CAD, rapid prototyping, or even offshore manufacturing but that empathic, intuitive, pattern-recognizing, parallel-processing, and neural-networking Internet that each of us carries between our ears. For the time being, at any rate, it is our ability to construct complex concepts that are both functionally relevant and emotionally resonant that sets humans apart from the ever more sophisticated machines we use to assist us. As long as there is no algorithm that will tell us how to bring divergent possibilities into a convergent reality or analytical detail into a synthetic whole, this talent will guarantee that accomplished design thinkers have a place in the world.

People may be deterred from venturing into the turbulent world of design thinking for any number of reasons. They may believe that creativity is an inner gift possessed only by celebrity designers, that it is better just to gaze respectfully at their chairs and lamps in modern art museums. Or they may suppose that it is a skill reserved for a priesthood of trained professionals—after all, we hire "designers" to do everything from cutting our hair to decorating our houses. Others, less in awe of the cult of the designer, may confuse the mastery of tools—including the qualitative tools of brainstorming, visual thinking, and storytelling—with the ability to reach a design solution. And there are those who may feel that without a precise framework or methodology, they will be unable to fathom what is going on. They are the ones who are most likely to bail out when the morale of a team dips, as it invariably will over the life of a project. What they may not appreciate is that design thinking is neither art nor science nor religion. It is the capacity, ultimately, for *integrative* thinking.

As dean of the acclaimed Rotman School of Management at the University of Toronto, Roger Martin is well positioned to observe the world's great managerial leaders and in particular the ability shared by many of them to hold multiple ideas in tension to reach new solutions. In *The Opposable Mind*, based on more than fifty in-depth interviews, Martin argues that "thinkers who exploit opposing ideas to construct a new solution enjoy a built-in advantage over thinkers who can consider only one model at a time." Integrative thinkers know how to widen the scope of issues salient to the problem. They resist the "either/or" in favor of the "both/and" and see nonlinear and multidirectional relationships as a source of inspiration, not contradiction. The most successful leaders, Martin finds, "embrace the mess." They allow complexity to exist, at least as they search for solutions, because complexity is the most reliable source of creative opportunities. The traits of management leaders, in other words, match the traits I have ascribed to design thinkers. This is no coincidence, and it does not imply that the "opposable mind" is the reward to those who won the genetic lottery. The skills that make for a great design thinker—the ability to spot patterns in the mess of complex inputs; to synthesize new ideas from fragmented parts; to empathize with people different from ourselves—can all be learned.

One day, perhaps, neurobiologists will be able to plug us into an MRI scanner and determine which parts of the brain light up when we apply integrative thinking. That may make it easier to devise new strategies for teaching people how to do it better. For the moment, at least, our task is not to understand what is going on in our brains but to find ways of getting that thinking out into the world, where it can be shared with others and, ultimately, translated into concrete strategies.

# building to think,

## or *the power of prototyping*

Lego launched me on my career as a design thinker. In the early 1970s, when I was nine or ten, England was going through yet another of its periodic recessions and the coal miners had waited until winter to go out on strike. This meant no coal for the power stations, which meant not enough electricity to meet demand, which meant regular blackouts. Determined to do my bit, I marshaled my entire inventory of Legos and built a great big flashlight using some fancy light bricks that glowed in the dark. I proudly handed the flashlight to my mother so that she had enough light to cook my dinner. I had built my first prototype.

By the age of ten I had learned the power of prototyping based on years of intensive study. As a younger child I had spent hours using Legos and Meccano (known to Americans as Erector Sets) to create a world full of rocket ships, dinosaurs, and robots of every imaginable size and shape. Like every other kid, I was thinking with my hands, using physical props as a springboard for my imagination. This shift from physical to abstract and back again is one of the most fundamental processes by which we explore the universe, unlock our imaginations, and open our minds to new possibilities.

Most companies are full of people who have set aside such childish pursuits and moved on to more important matters such as writing reports and filling out forms, but one thing strikes the visitor to an organization that uses design thinking: as in any child's bedroom, there are prototypes everywhere. Peek inside a project room, and you will see prototypes on every surface. Walk the halls, and you will see prototypes being used to tell stories about past projects. You will see prototyping tools ranging from X-acto knives and masking tape to $50,000 laser cutters. Whatever the budget and whatever the facilities, prototyping will be the essence of the place.

Frank Lloyd Wright claimed that his early childhood experience with Froebel kindergarten blocks—developed by Friedrich Froebel in the 1830s to help children learn the principles of geometry—ignited his creative passion: "The maplewood blocks . . . are in my fingers to this day," he wrote in his autobiography. Charles and Ray Eames, one of the greatest prototyping teams of all times, used prototyping to explore and refine ideas, sometimes over many years. The result was nothing short of the reinvention of twentieth-century furniture. Asked by a curious admirer whether the iconic Eames lounge chair came to him in a flash, Charles replied, "Yes, sort of a thirty-year flash."

Since openness to experimentation is the lifeblood of any creative organization, prototyping—the willingness to go ahead and try something by building it—is the best evidence of experimentation. We may think of a prototype as a finished model of a product about to be manufactured, but that definition should be carried much further back in the process. It needs to include studies that may appear rough and simple and encompass more than just physical objects. Furthermore, it's not necessary to be an industrial designer to adopt the habit of prototyping: financial services executives, retail merchants, hospital administrators, city planners, and transportation engineers can and should participate in this essential component of design thinking, as we shall see. David Kelley calls prototyping "thinking with your hands," and he contrasts it with specification-led, planning-driven abstract thinking. Both have value and each has its place, but one is much more effective at creating new ideas and driving them forward.

## quick and dirty

Although it might seem as though frittering away valuable time on sketches and models and simulations will slow work down, prototyping generates results *faster.* This seems counterintuitive: surely it takes longer to *build* an idea than to *think* one? Perhaps, but only for those gifted few who are able to think the right idea the first time. Most problems worth worrying about are complex, and a series of early experiments is often the best way to decide among competing directions. The faster we make our ideas tangible, the sooner we will be able to evaluate them, refine them, and zero in on the best solution.

Gyrus ACMI is on the cutting edge of surgical instrumentation and a leader in developing techniques for minimally invasive surgery. In 2001 IDEO began to work with Gyrus to develop a new apparatus for operating on delicate nasal tissues. Early on in the project the team met with six otolaryngology surgeons to learn how they performed the procedure, the problems with existing instruments, and what characteristics they might be looking for in a new system. One of the surgeons, using imprecise words and awkward hand gestures, described how he might prefer a device with a pistol grip. After they departed one of our designers had grabbed a whiteboard marker and a 35 mm film canister and taped them to a plastic clothespin that was lying nearby, and squeezed the clothespin as if it were a trigger. This rudimentary prototype catapulted the discussion forward, put everyone on the same page, and saved countless meetings, videoconferences, shop time, and airplane tickets. Cost of the prototype in labor and materials: $0 (we were able to rescue the marking pen).

Just as it can accelerate the pace of a project, prototyping allows the exploration of many ideas in parallel. Early prototypes should be fast, rough, and cheap. The greater the investment in an idea, the more committed one becomes to it. Overinvestment in a refined prototype has two undesirable consequences: First, a mediocre idea may go too far toward realization—or even, in the worst case, all the way. Second, the prototyping process itself creates the opportunity to discover new and better ideas at minimal cost. Product designers can use cheap and easy-to-manipulate materials: cardboard, surfboard foam, wood, and even objects and materials they find lying around—anything they can glue or tape or staple together to create a physical approximation of ideas. IDEO's first and greatest prototype was created when the company consisted of eight scruffy designers crowded together in a studio above Roxy's dress shop on University Avenue in Palo Alto. Douglas Dayton and Jim Yurchenco affixed the roller ball from a tube of Ban Roll-on deodorant to the base of a plastic butter dish. Before long Apple Computer was shipping its first mouse.

## enough is enough

Prototypes should command only as much time, effort, and investment as is necessary to generate useful feedback and drive an idea forward. The greater the complexity and expense, the more "finished" it is likely to seem and the less likely its creators will be to profit from constructive feedback—or even to listen to it. The goal of prototyping is not to create a working model. It is to give form to an idea to learn about its strengths and weaknesses and to identify new directions for the next generation of more detailed, more refined prototypes. A prototype's scope should be limited. The purpose of early prototypes might be to understand whether an idea has functional value. Eventually designers need to take the prototype out into the world to get feedback from the intended users of the final product. At this point the surface qualities of the prototype may require a bit more attention so that potential consumers are not distracted by the rough edges or unresolved details. Most people, for example, will find it difficult to visualize how a washing machine made of cardboard will work.

Some pretty amazing technology is available today for designers to create prototypes quickly and at an extremely high level of fidelity, including ultraprecise laser cutters, computer-aided design tools, and machines that function as 3-D printers. Sometimes they are too good, as we discovered when a Steelcase executive, mistaking an expertly detailed foam model for the real thing, destroyed a $40,000 prototype of the Vecta chair by sitting on it. But all the technology in the world will come to naught if it is used to create prototypes too refined, too detailed, and too early. "Just enough prototyping" means picking what we want to learn about and achieving just enough resolution to make that the focus. An experienced prototyper knows when to say "Enough is enough."

## prototyping things you can't pick up

Most imaginable prototypes up to this point refer to physical products—stuff that hurts when you trip over it or drop it on your toes. The same rules apply when the challenge is a service, a virtual experience, or even an organizational system.

Anything tangible that lets us explore an idea, evaluate it, and push it forward is a prototype. I have seen sophisticated insulin injection devices that began life as Legos. I have seen software interfaces mocked up with Post-it notes long before a line of code was written. I have seen new concepts for neighborhood banking acted out before clients as a skit, against a backdrop of "counters" made of flimsy foam core—a kind of cardboard material that is very strong, very light, and very cheap—held together with masking tape. In each case an idea has been given expression through an appropriate medium to show to others for feedback.

The movie industry has long used this practice. Once upon a time, when film was little more than a recorded version of theater, it was feasible to go from a script straight to shooting the movie. But as directors grew more ambitious—and audiences more demanding—they began to include multiple cameras and special effects. The storyboard emerged as a way of mapping out the movie before it was shot to make sure that all the scenes were thought through and that the director wouldn't get to the editing room only to find a vital angle or crucial shot flawed or missing. As filmmaking grew ever more sophisticated, especially pioneered by Walt Disney Studios' animation, the storyboard took on an even more important role. It became a prototyping tool that enabled animators to assure themselves that the story hung together before the detail work began. Today, with sophisticated, expensive digital special effects dominating so much of Hollywood, filmmakers have moved to computer-based storyboards and "animatics" to test the motion in a shot before they commit to the real thing.

Techniques borrowed from film and other creative industries suggest how we might prototype nonphysical experiences. These include scenarios, a form of storytelling in which some potential future situation or state is described using words and pictures. We might, for example, invent a character who fits a set of demographic factors that interest us—a divorced professional woman with two small children, for instance—and develop a believable scenario around her daily routine in order to "observe" how she might use an electric vehicle charger or an online pharmacy.

When Wi-Fi communications were in their infancy, Vocera developed a video scenario to demonstrate how employees might use a wearable, voice-controlled "communications badge" to stay connected with coworkers anywhere within a company's network. The short movie followed the rounds of a fictional IT support team and was far more effective in explaining the concept to potential investors than a technical brief or a deck of PowerPoint slides. Sony used the same technique when it was developing its first online concepts in the early 1990s. A design team created scenarios around the lives of teenagers in

Tokyo to show how they might use new kinds of online gaming parlors to play interactive video games or sing karaoke songs together. In the early years of the Internet these plausible fictions helped management visualize how it might become the basis of new services and business models.

Another considerable value of scenarios is that they force us to keep people at the center of the idea, preventing us from getting lost in mechanical or aesthetic details. They remind us at every moment that we are not dealing with things but with what the psychologist Mihaly Csikszentmihalyi calls *"transactions between people and things."* Prototyping at work is giving form to an idea, allowing us to learn from it, evaluate it against others, and improve upon it.

A simple scenario structure useful in the development of new services is the "customer journey." This structure charts the stages through which an imagined customer passes from the beginning of a service experience to the end. The starting point may be imaginary, or it may come directly from observations of people purchasing an airline ticket or deciding whether or not to install solar panels on a roof. In either case, the value of describing a customer journey is that it clarifies where the customer and the service or brand interact. Every one of these "touchpoints" points to an opportunity to provide value to a firm's intended customers—or to derail them for good.

Some years ago Amtrak began studying opportunities to improve transportation on the East Coast by offering a high-speed train service between Boston, New York, and Washington, D.C. By the time Amtrak invited IDEO to participate in what would become the Acela project, the focus had narrowed to the trains themselves and, in fact, to the design of the seats.

After spending countless days riding trains with customers, the team created a simple customer journey that described the entire travel process. The journey, for most customers, had ten steps, which included getting to the station, finding parking, buying tickets, locating the platform, and so on. The insight that proved most striking was that passengers did not take their seats on the train until stage eight—most of the experience of train travel, in other words, did not involve the train at all. The team reasoned that every one of the prior steps was an opportunity to create a positive interaction, opportunities that would have been overlooked if they had focused only on the design of the seats. Admittedly, this approach made the project far more complex, but that is typical in the move from design to design thinking. It may not be easy to reconcile the many interests that come into play in getting from Washington to New York, but Amtrak managed to do so and has created a more complete and satisfying experience for its customers. Despite its numerous and well-publicized problems with tracks, brake systems, and wheel sets, Acela has proved to be a popular service. The customer journey was the first prototype in that process.

## acting out

If playing with Legos is a child's way of "learning with your hands" and foam core and computer-driven milling machines are the equivalent for grown-up product designers, what does it look like for service innovation—the experience a person may have at a bank, a clinic, or the Department of Motor Vehicles? Our most reliable consultants, here as with so many other products, are kids. As soon as two or three children get together, they start to role-play: they become doctors and nurses, pirates, aliens, or Disney characters. Without prompting, they begin to perform lengthy enactments full of complex plots and subplots. Research suggests that this form of play is not only fun but also helps establish internal scripts by which we navigate as adults.

TownePlace Suites, an extended-stay hotel brand owned by Marriott, serves business travelers, such as consultants with long-term contracts, who may be required to be away from home for more than just a few nights and want to feel more at home than is usually the case in hotels. They are likely to work in their rooms more regularly, they stay over on weekends, and they may spend time on their own exploring the neighborhood. Marriott wanted to rethink the highly specific experience of these travelers.

Traditionally, one of the problems with architectural design is that full-scale prototyping is virtually impossible because it is just too expensive. Instead, an imaginative team of "space designers" rented an old warehouse in a dicey part of San Francisco's Bayview district, where they built a full-scale mock-up of the entrance lobby and a typical guest suite of foam core. Their mock-up was not intended to showcase the aesthetic qualities of the space. Rather, it served as a stage on which designers, the client team, a group of hotel owner-operators, and even "customers" could act out different service experiences and explore in real space and real time what felt right. All the visitors were encouraged to add Post-its to the prototype and to suggest changes. This process yielded a host of innovations that included personalized guidebooks with local information tailored to repeat clients and their specific needs as well as a huge wall map in the lobby where guests could use magnetic tiles to mark interesting restaurants or other landmarks—a sort of "open-source guestbook." This full-scale space for acting out whatever occurred to them gave the design team a rich set of ideas for further testing. Moreover, they had a much better sense of how good the ideas were. No amount of survey work or virtual simulation would have achieved the same result,

Learning to feel comfortable acting out potential ideas is obviously important for anyone contemplating an experiential approach to prototyping—Mattel's Ivy Ross went so far as to teach new recruits to the Platypus program how to use improvisational acting techniques in the first couple of weeks of the session. Knowing some of the basics, such as how to build on the ideas of one's fellow actors and being willing to defer judgment of them, increases the likelihood that collaborative, real-time prototyping will be successful. The amateur theatrics of an experiential prototype can look foolish. It takes a certain confidence for individuals to loosen their ties, slip off their heels, and explore an idea through improvisation.

## prototyping in the wild

Most prototyping takes place behind closed doors, for obvious reasons. It is often necessary to protect the confidentiality of ideas and limit their exposure so that the competition (and sometimes management) doesn't know what's up. Traditional companies may arrange focus groups or customer clinics, and edgier companies such as Electronic Arts regularly bring in gamers to test their games during development. Controlled environments such as these work well enough in evaluating a product's functional characteristics: Does it work? Will it break when dropped? How well do the parts fit together? Will an average person be able to find the on/off switch? In fact, these are often aspects of a product that can be tested by the project team members themselves. Things become more complicated with services, however, and particularly with services that rely on complex social interactions. Mobile telephony, for example, draws on intangible interactions of users with one another and with the system itself. Today's complex ideas require prototypes to be released into the wild to see how they survive and adapt.

When the German mobile phone company T-Mobile began exploring ways of creating social groups via mobile phones, the company believed that networks of like-minded individuals could use phones not just to stay in touch but to share pictures and messages, make plans, synchronize schedules, and facilitate a hundred other interactions in a much more immediate way than with a PC. It would have been possible to create scenarios and storyboards to describe T-Mobile's ideas, and even to create simulations to run on phones. But the *social* dimension of the problem would have been overlooked. The only way to achieve this was to launch a prototype service. The design team loaded two prototypes onto some Nokia phones and handed them out to small groups of users in Slovakia and the Czech Republic. In less than two weeks it was clear which of the two prototypes was more compelling and why. The winning idea—helping users build social networks around events in their calendars—surprised the team, which had favored the alternative idea—helping people to create shared phone books. By launching prototypes, the team not only gathered real evidence of how the new service might be used but avoided chasing after its own less promising idea. There was only one flaw in the innovative methodology: at the end of the trial, several of the users refused to give back their phones.

Another emerging form of "prototyping in the wild" involves the use of virtual worlds such as Second Life or social networks such as MySpace and Facebook. Companies can learn from consumers about proposed brands or services before they invest in the real thing. One successful example is the Starwood hotel chain, which launched a 3-D, computer-generated prototype of its planned Aloft brand inside the virtual world of Second Life in October 2006. Over the next nine months virtual guests inundated Starwood with suggestions on everything from the overall layout down to putting radios in the showers and repainting the lobby in earth tones. When enough feedback had been collected, Starwood shut down the virtual hotel to "renovate." When it reopened, a gala cyberparty erupted in which hip avatars danced in the lobby, flirted in the bar, and hung out around the pool. And what do you do with an expensive virtual prototype once real construction begins? Starwood donated its abandoned "sim" to the online youth empowerment group TakingITGlobal.

Starwood's Aloft brand wanted to capture a youthful, urban, stylish, and tech-savvy clientele—just the types likely to be found cruising the neighborhoods of Second Life. But the advantages of virtual prototyping make it likely that other, more conservative businesses will begin to experiment with it. Virtual prototyping allows companies to reach prospective customers quickly and get feedback from people in numerous locations. Iterations are easy, and as more of them begin to explore the prototyping potential of online social networking, we will become increasingly adept at evaluating them. Like any prototyping medium, however, there are limitations. Virtual worlds such as Second Life rely upon avatars that represent customers, but we have no idea who they really are. This can be risky, as things are not always as they appear.

## minding your own business

It is one thing to talk about prototyping material objects and even intangible services, but there is also a role for prototyping more abstract challenges, such as the design of new business strategies, new business offerings, and even new business organizations. Prototypes may bring an abstract idea to life in a way that a whole organization can understand and engage with.

HBO, famous for bringing us shows such as *The Sopranos* and *Sex and the City*, had by 2004 come to realize that the TV landscape was changing. It had earned its dominance in cable TV by delivering premium content, but the company could see that new delivery platforms such as Internet TV, mobile telephony, and video on demand were destined to become more important. HBO wanted to understand what the impact of these changes might be.

After a lengthy process of research and consumer observation, a strategy emerged based on creating seamless content that would spread across all of the emerging new technology platforms: desktop PCs, laptops, mobile phones, and Internet protocol television (IPTV). HBO, we concluded, should be willing to loosen its identification with cable TV and become "technology agnostic," bringing content to customers whenever they wanted it and wherever they were. Instead of making a TV program and then thinking about what to do with DVDs or mobile content, shows should be created with these other channels in mind from the outset. We understood that this ambitious agenda challenged some fundamental premises. It required HBO not only to gain a deeper understanding of how audiences relate to media but also to break down some of the entrenched silos that existed within the company itself.

To create a compelling vision of the customer experience, the project team built prototypes and installed them in a walkthrough experience on the fifteenth floor of HBO's New York headquarters. This enabled senior executives to see firsthand how customers might interact with TV content that they could access from different devices. For technical and analytical grounding, they constructed a future road map that ran the entire length of a wall and displayed the elements of technology, business, and culture that the company would confront as the program moved forward. Touring the fifteenth-floor environment we'd created, Eric Kessler, vice president for Marketing, got it: "This isn't about the future of HBO On Demand. It's about the future of HBO."

The prototype projected HBO management into the future in a compelling, realistic way, helping them visualize both the opportunities and the challenges to come. When HBO entered into discussions with Cingular (which is now AT&T Wireless) to put premium TV content onto a mobile platform, the fifteenth-floor prototype helped them to reach a common understanding.

## phase shift: prototyping an organization

HBO illustrates the need to think with our hands even when working at the level of business strategy, and the same is true for the design of organizations themselves. Institutions must evolve with changing environments. Though the company "re-org" has become a cliché in business culture, it is neverthe- less one of the most fateful and complex design problems any company may face, though it is rarely accompanied by any of the basic characteristics of good design thinking. Meetings are called in which there is no brainstorming; organizational charts are drawn up with little evidence of any thinking with the hands; plans are made and directives are issued without the benefit of prototyping. I don't know if IDEO could have saved the American auto industry, but we would have started with foam core and a hot glue gun.

To be sure, prototyping new organizational structures is difficult. By their nature, they are suspended in webs of inter- connectedness. No unit can be tinkered with without affecting other parts of the organization. Prototyping with peoples' lives is also a delicate proposition because there is, rightly, less toler- ance for error. But despite this complexity, some institutions have taken a designer's approach to organizational change.

The implosion of the dot-com supernova at the end of 2000 created a black hole whose epicenter was the San Francisco Bay Area. Designerly lofts were abandoned throughout San Francisco's "Multimedia Gulch," leaving only Aeron chairs and colorful iMacs; the $100,000-a-month billboards along Highway 101, the main corridor through Silicon Valley, fell empty; would-be entrepreneurs returned to college to finish their degrees. IDEO, which had been working with new start-ups while helping more established companies navigate the passage into the Internet age, was hit hard. For the first time in our history, we experienced a forced belt-tightening. I had been summoned back from the United Kingdom, where I was head-ing up IDEO's European operations to take over the reins of leadership from David Kelley, who, with his exquisite sense of timing, had decided to step down just minutes (or so it seemed) before the e-bubble burst, to focus on his academic life at Stan-ford. It fell to me to oversee the transition to IDEO 2.0.

From a company that had once boasted that it would never grow beyond forty employees (so that we could lock the front door, jump onto a school bus, and drive to the beach), we had now expanded nearly tenfold, and although we worked hard to preserve a flat organizational structure, that growth translated into 350 careers, benefits packages, and dreams to fulfill. The stakes were high and there was no safety net, so I decided to do what designers do: I put together a team, and we launched a project. The brief? To reinvent the firm.

Having spent the previous two decades creating a human-centered design process for our clients, it would have been odd indeed if we had not applied it to ourselves. That is precisely what we did. During "Phase One" the project team fanned out across the landscape, talking to designers in each of our offices, our clients, our network of collaborators, and even our com-petitors to gain insight into how the field was evolving, where we were weak, and where we were strong. These discussions led to a series of workshops and our first prototypes, which took the form of a cluster of "Big Ideas" that captured the future as we saw it. One of these was the idea of "design with a small d"—using design as a tool to improve the quality of life at every level, as opposed to creating the signature *objets* that grace the pedestals of art museums and the covers of lifestyle magazines. Another was the idea we called "One IDEO," the notion that our future depended on our acting not as independent studios but as a single interconnected network. A third idea was to abandon our original "studio" model—which reflected the way designers are organized—and replace it with a new, untested structure of "global practices" intended to reflect the way the world itself is organized: the "Health Practice" would focus on projects from precision medical equipment for Medtronic to educational packaging for GlaxoSmithKline; "Zero20" on the needs of kids from early infancy through late adolescence; other practices would be focused around interactive software, consumer experiences, the design of "smart spaces," and even organizational transformation. At this point we felt that we were ready to take our prototypes out into the field. Or, to be more precise, we took the field to the prototypes.

We decided to stage a global event that, for the first time since we had expanded beyond our base in Silicon Valley, would bring together every employee of IDEO in one place: senior mechanical engineers from Boston, newly hired graphic designers from London, model makers from San Francisco, human factors specialists from Tokyo, and even our beloved receptionist Vicky in Palo Alto converged upon the Bay Area to jump-start what we soon began to call IDEO 2.0. Standing up in front of that audience of 350 peers, colleagues, and mentors to launch the event remains the high point of my career. Little did I know that the kickoff was the easy bit.

The launch—three days of lectures, seminars, workshops,

dancing, and a mass version of the old computer game Pong with 350 simultaneous players—was a huge success. The following year, however, was one of the toughest I have ever experienced. As the prototypes unfolded, we learned that a story needs to be repeated many times before people understand how it applies to them and many more times again before they change their behavior. We learned that leadership teams that had been successful with small local groups might not easily project their ideas across seven locations. We learned that visionary designers who had been accustomed to complete creative autonomy did not happily adapt to the idea of market-driven practices.

We redesigned IDEO because we wanted the organization to remain flexible, nimble, relevant, and responsive to the new global environment that was taking shape. Five years on, two of the original seven practices no longer exist, a new one has been added, and one has refashioned and renamed itself twice to find better resonance with its intended clients. When it comes to organizations, constant change is inevitable and everything is a prototype. At the most challenging times we reminded ourselves that a successful prototype is not one that works flawlessly; it is one that teaches us something—about our objectives, our process, and ourselves.

There are many approaches to prototyping, but they share a single, paradoxical feature: They slow us down to speed us up. By taking the time to prototype our ideas, we avoid costly mistakes such as becoming too complex too early and sticking with a weak idea for too long.

I wrote earlier that all design thinkers, whether or not they happen to have been trained in any of the recognized design disciplines, inhabit three "spaces of innovation." Since design thinkers will continue to "think with their hands" throughout the life of a project—aiming toward greater fidelity as it advances toward completion—prototyping is one of the practices that enable them to occupy all three realms simultaneously.

Prototyping is always *inspirational*—not in the sense of a perfected artwork but just the opposite: because it inspires new ideas. Prototyping should start early in the life of a project, and we expect them to be numerous, quickly executed, and pretty ugly. Each one is intended to develop an idea "just enough" to allow the team to learn something and move on. At this relatively low level of resolution, it's almost always best for the team members to make their own prototypes and not outsource them to others. Designers may require a fully equipped model shop, but *design thinkers* can "build" prototypes in the cafeteria, a boardroom, or a hotel suite.

One way to motivate early-stage prototyping is to set a goal: to have a prototype ready by the end of the first week or even the first day. Once tangible expressions begin to emerge, it becomes easy to try them out and elicit feedback internally from management and externally from potential customers. Indeed, one of the measures of an innovative organization is its average time to first prototype. In some organizations, this work can take months or even years—the automobile industry is a telling example. In the most creative organizations, it can happen within a few days.

In the *ideation* space we build prototypes to develop our

ideas to ensure that they incorporate the functional and emotional elements necessary to meet the demands of the market. As the project moves forward, the number of prototypes will go down while the resolution of each one goes up, but the purpose remains the same: to help refine an idea and improve it. If the precision required at this stage exceeds the capabilities of the team, it may be necessary to turn to outside experts—model makers, videographers, writers, or actors, as the case may be—for help.

In the third space of innovation we are concerned with *implementation*: communicating an idea with sufficient clarity to gain acceptance across the organization, proving it, and showing that it will work in its intended market. Here too, the habit of prototyping plays an essential role. At different stages the prototype may serve to validate a subassembly of a subassembly: the graphics on a screen, the armrest of a chair, or a detail in the interaction between a blood donor and a Red Cross volunteer. As the project nears completion, prototypes will likely be more complete. They will probably be expensive and complex and may be indistinguishable from the real thing. By this time you know you have a good idea; you just don't yet know how good it is.

McDonald's is a company famous for applying the prototyping process throughout each of the spaces of innovation. In the *inspirational* space, designers use sketches, quick mock-ups, and scenarios to explore new services, product offerings, and customer experiences. These might be kept under wraps or shown to management or consumers to get early feedback. To nurture the *ideation* space, McDonald's has built a sophisticated prototyping facility at its headquarters outside Chicago where project teams can configure every type of cooking equipment, point-of-sale technology, and restaurant layout to test new ideas. When a new idea is almost ready for *implementation*, it will often be tested in the form of a pilot deployed at selected restaurants.

# returning to the surface,

## or *the design of experiences*

I fly between San Francisco and New York too often, but it's a trip I enjoy making. Coming from Britain, New York represents iconic America for me. It was the first U.S. city that I visited, and I always experience a twinge of excitement at the prospect of a return. Not so long ago, however, the flight was something that just had to be tolerated. The sum total of old airplanes, cramped space, miserable food, poor entertainment systems, inconvenient schedules, and indifferent service stripped away what should be the incomparable magic of flight.

In 2004, still reeling from the aftermath of 9/11, United Airlines introduced a new service on the San Francisco–New York route called p.s. (for "Premium Service") that attempted to solve some of these issues. In a stroke, United leapfrogged its competitors. Most of the cabin of the 757s was converted to business seats, since the vast majority of the customers on this route are business travelers. Legroom was increased measurably, but the new configuration also created a feeling of roominess in the cabin. United introduced better food service and provided personalized DVD players to its business passengers.

These improvements helped set United p.s. apart from its competitors, but there was one aspect of the new service that particularly transformed the experience for me as a passenger:

the added floor space altered the boarding experience. Not only did I now have plenty of space to stow my gear without getting in the way of fellow passengers, but that deadly twenty- or thirty-minute interval between boarding and takeoff became a *social* experience. On almost every flight I would find myself chatting with my neighbors without impatient passengers trying to squeeze past. Even before the doors closed and our tray tables were "returned to the upright position," United had managed to make boarding the aircraft a social experience that set my expectations for the remainder of the flight. The net effect reinforced the sense of excitement and anticipation I feel when I travel. The experience makes a connection to my emotions and not just to my schedule.

Buried in my experience with the corporate jet set is one of the most complex challenges facing any organization committed to the principles of design thinking: when we sit on an airplane, shop for groceries, or check into a hotel, we are not only carrying out a function but having an experience. That function can be compromised if the experience attending it is not designed with the same mindfulness a good engineer brings to a product or an architect to a building. This chapter turns to the design of experiences, examining three themes that make experiences meaningful and memorable: First, we now live in what Joseph Pine and James Gilmore christened an "experience economy" in which people shift from passive consumption to active participation. Second, the best experiences are not scripted at corporate headquarters but delivered on the spot by service providers. And third, implementation is everything. An experience must be as finely crafted and precision-engineered as any other product.

# a good idea is no longer enough

Innovation has been defined as "a good idea executed well." This is a good start. Unfortunately, too much emphasis falls on the first half of that proposition. I have seen countless examples of good ideas that never gained traction for the simple reason of poor execution. Most of them never reach the market, and those that do end up littering the stockrooms of electronics stores and supermarkets.

New products or services may be doomed for all sorts of reasons: uneven quality, unimaginative marketing, unreliable distribution, or unrealistic pricing. Even when all the metrics and mechanics of business are in place, however, a poorly executed idea will most likely fail. The problem may lie with the physical design of the product—too big, too heavy, too complex. Likewise, the touchpoints for a new service—the retail space or software interface—may not connect to consumers. These are failures of design, and they can usually be fixed. Increasingly, however, ideas fail because people demand more of them than reliable performance in an acceptable package. The components of a product need to come together to create a great experience. This is a much more complicated proposition.

There have been many explanations for this new level of heightened expectation. Among the most compelling is Daniel Pink's analysis of what might be called the psychodynamics of affluence. In *A Whole New Mind*, Pink argues that once our basic needs are met—as they already have been for most people in the affluent societies of the West—we tend to look for meaningful and emotionally satisfying experiences.

We need only note the disproportionate growth of the service—entertainment, banking, health care—economies relative to manufacturing. Moreover, these services themselves have gone far beyond the support of basic needs: Hollywood movies, video games, gourmet restaurants, continuing education, ecotourism, and destination shopping have grown dramatically in recent years. Their value lies in the emotional resonance they create.

The Walt Disney Company may be the clearest example of an experience business, and we should not assume that it is only about entertainment. Experiences are deeper and more meaningful. They imply active participation, not passive consumption, which can happen on many different levels. Sitting with your three-year-old daughter as she sings along with *The Little Mermaid* is an experience that goes well beyond entertainment. A family trip to Disney World may be quite stressful—the food is terrible, the lines are too long, and the youngest sibling will melt down when she's told that she's too short to go on Space Mountain—but most visitors remember it as one of the great experiences of family life.

The real meaning of the "experience economy," then, is not primarily entertainment. The hierarchy of value they describe in their influential book—from commodities to products to services to experiences—corresponds to a fundamental shift in how we experience the world, from the primarily functional to the primarily emotional. Understanding this shift, many companies now invest in the delivery of experiences. Functional benefits alone, it seems, are no longer enough to capture customers or create the brand distinction to retain them.

# from consumption to participation

The industrial revolution created not just consumers but a consumer society. The sheer scale required to sustain the economics of industrialization meant that not only did products become standardized but so did the services associated with them. This brought tremendous benefits to society, including lower prices, higher quality, and improved living standards. The downside was that over time the role of consumers became almost entirely passive.

The English reformers who invented modern design at the end of the nineteenth century were acutely aware of this. They foresaw a world in which the torrent of cheap goods pouring out of Britain's factories no longer held any connection to the workers who made them or meaning for the public that purchased them. William Morris, the larger-than-life force behind the English Arts and Crafts Movement, was the most articulate spokesman for the view that the industrial revolution had ushered in a world of unimaginable riches but one drained of feeling, passion, and deep human engagement: "Think of it!" he thundered at the end of his life. "Was it all to end in a counting house on top of a cinder-heap?"

An unapologetic romantic, Morris believed that industrialization had severed art from utility, had opened up a gulf between "useful work and useless toil," had contaminated the natural environment in the pursuit of goods, and had degraded what ought to have been a celebration of the human capacity to enjoy the fruits of our labor. Morris died in 1896, feeling that he had failed in his mission to reconcile the seemingly contradictory claims of objects and experiences. He lamented that his fellow craftsmen had become little more than "a tiresome little aristocracy working with high skill for the very rich." Almost in spite of themselves, however, they set the agenda that would drive design theory in the twentieth century.

Today we still wrestle with creating meaningful experiences out of the sheer glut of products—informational, now, as much as industrial—that threaten to consume us even as we consume them. Lawrence Lessig, a professor of law and the founder of the Stanford Center for Internet and Society, might be surprised to see himself compared to William Morris, but in his efforts to wrest control of our creative energies in the age of Big Media, he is continuing Morris's campaign against Big Industry and partaking of the same great tradition of using design as a tool of social reform. In a steady stream of books, lectures, and online discourses, Lessig has shown how we moved from a preindustrial world in which most of us were producers to an industrial world in which we have mostly become consumers of mass-produced media—a reversal traceable in many industries. Unlike his Victorian predecessor, however, who gazed backward toward a hopelessly idealized vision of the medieval craftsman producing his own goods, Lessig looks forward to a postindustrial digital age in which we will once again create our own experiences.

Lessig uses the example of music to show how we are moving back to active participation in our experiences from the passive consumption of the late twentieth century. Prior to the invention of radio and the phonograph, composers sold their scores to publishing houses, which in turn sold them, in the form of sheet music, to customers who played the music themselves—at home, at family gatherings, and so on. With the emergence of the new broadcast media technologies, we stopped *playing* music at home every evening and started *listening* to it: first on our radios and phonographs and eventually on stereos, boom boxes, and Walkmans. With the emergence of digital music and the Internet, however, many more of us are once again making music instead of merely consuming it. We now have software tools that enable us to grab music from the Web, create mixes, samples, and mash-ups, and redistribute the results. Applications like Apple's Garage Band allow us to create music without formal training or even the ability to play instruments, with the result that seven-year-olds can now create unique sound tracks for the PowerPoint presentations they make for their school reports.

The campaigns of William Morris and Lawrence Lessig, separated by a century, an ocean, and another technology revolution, indicate the perceptual shift we will have to make as designers of experiences. Just as Web 1.0 blasted information at prospective customers whereas Web 2.0 is all about engaging them, companies now know they can no longer treat people as passive consumers. We have seen in previous chapters how the shift to participatory design is fast becoming the norm in the development of new products. The same is true of experiences.

Design has the power to enrich our lives by engaging our emotions through image, form, texture, color, sound, and smell. The intrinsically human-centered nature of *design thinking* points to the next step: we can use our empathy and understanding of people to design experiences that create opportunities for active engagement and participation.

## experience engineering

Though Disney may be the most powerful example of experiences at scale—Disneyland in Anaheim can easily welcome 100,000 visitors in a single day—we now see a growing number of brands whose proposition is also based on participatory experiences. The food industry offers perhaps the most dramatic example of a category being transformed both at the source of production and the point of distribution. Through the 1950s and '60s, in Europe and America, local stores began to disappear, replaced by inexpensive but sterile supermarkets. The drive to lower prices—through such industrial processes as packaging, chemical preservatives, refrigeration, storage, and long-distance transport—not only removed much of the natural quality from food but also dehumanized an experience that lies close to the origins of human society. The growing popularity of farmers' markets, community-supported agriculture, the slow-food movement, and a burgeoning literature ranging from Michael Pollan's *In Defense of Food* to Barbara Kingsolver's *Animal, Vegetable, Miracle*, suggests that consumers crave a different experience of food shopping.

Earlier on I discussed the popularity of Whole Foods Market, one of the most successful retailers in the United States. Whole Foods Market continues to grow not just because of the growing market for organics but because it appreciates the importance of experience. Every aspect of the stores—the fresh produce displays, the free samples, the wealth of information about the preparation and storage of food, the variety of "healthy lifestyle" products—is designed to draw us in, to invite us to linger and *participate*. In the flagship store in Austin, Texas, Whole Foods has even experimented with allowing customers to cook.

Experience brands raise the bar when it comes to engaging with the customer at every possible opportunity. Virgin America is an experience brand, as attested by its Web site, its service interactions, and its advertising, all of which ease us into the check-in experience and the actual in-flight service. United is not. Though the p.s. service may be great, no other aspect of the airline reinforces the experience proposition. Experiments abound, however, and we may find them in some unexpected places.

The famed Mayo Clinic in Rochester, Minnesota, is an experience brand of an entirely different nature than Whole Foods Market, Virgin America, or Disney. Like many great hospitals, the Mayo is known worldwide for the expertise of its staff and the skill of its physicians at treating complex diseases. One way the institution sets itself apart from its competitors, however, is the manner in which it has extended its reputation for leading-edge research to innovation around the patient experience.

In 2002 a team of physicians headed by Drs. Nicholas LaRusso and Michael Brennan, the chair and associate chair of the Department of Medicine, respectively, approached IDEO with an idea for a laboratory of clinical experience. Might it be possible to construct an environment—an actual wing of the existing hospital facility—in which new approaches to patient care might be conceived, visualized, and prototyped? Using a set of principles that could have been lifted from a how-to manual of design thinking, we adapted our process to a methodology of "*See-Plan-Act-Refine-Communicate*" and embodied them in the state-of-the-art SPARC Innovation Program, which opened in 2004. We brought our process to the Mayo Clinic and left it there.

The SPARC laboratory is a design studio embedded in a clinical hospital (the former urology department, to be precise) in which designers, business strategists, medical and health professionals, *and patients* work in close proximity to develop ideas for improving the patient-provider experience. It operates in part like an experimental clinic, in part like an independent design consultancy for other units in the hospital. Half a dozen projects are going on at SPARC at any given time—from rethinking the traditional examination room to prototyping the interface of an electronic check-in kiosk. The work of the SPARC staff and affiliates seems destined to transform the patient experience throughout the institution.

From Disneyland to the Mayo Clinic, experiences can be created in the most playful and the most serious of categories. The example of SPARC suggests that design thinking can not only be applied to products and experiences but can be extended to the process of innovation itself.

## to change behaviors—or not to change

Many a frustrated brand manager (or politician or health advocate) has been heard venting that if only consumers (or voters or patients) would just change their behavior, everything would be okay. Unfortunately, getting people to change is difficult under the best of circumstances and all but impossible in the face of resistance.

One way to get people to try something new is to build on behaviors that are familiar to them, as we did when we tapped into the childhood memories of American adults to create a new cycling experience—coasting—for Shimano. An equally compelling story began when Bank of America came to IDEO to help generate product ideas that would help them retain current customers while at the same time bringing in new ones. The team generated about a dozen concepts—service ideas oriented toward boomer moms, educational tools to help parents teach their kids about responsible money management—but one seemed particularly to stick: a service that would help customers to save more. The first order of business was to understand people's prevailing behavior, so we donned our anthropologists' pith helmets and headed out into the field—to Baltimore, Atlanta, and San Francisco—to understand how saving figured in the lives of ordinary Americans.

We found that all people want to save more but only a few have strategies for doing so. At the same time, many people perform unconscious acts that suggest a promising direction. Some people, for example, routinely overpay their utility bills, either out of a love of round numbers or to make sure they are never surprised by a fee for a late payment. Another type of "invisible saving" is the habit of tossing our spare change into a jar at the end of the day (to the delight of the kids, who find it a bottomless source of allowance payments, and the dismay of bank tellers who have to count it out in exchange for a couple of dollars). The project team reasoned that it might be possible to build on these behavioral clues to encourage more saving.

The result, after numerous iterations, validations, and prototypes, was a new service launched by Bank of America in

October 2005, called "Keep the Change." Keep the Change automatically rounds up debit card purchases to the nearest dollar and transfers the difference into the customer's savings account. Now when I buy my morning latte at Peet's and pay my $3.50 with my debit card, the 50 cents change that I would have received if I had handed over $4.00 in cash is deposited in my savings account. With all the coffee I drink, the savings add up pretty quickly. I am not the only one to find this to be an easy way of saving. In its first year, Keep the Change attracted 2.5 million customers, which translates into more than 700,000 new checking accounts and 1 million new savings accounts. It is doubtful that results on this scale could have been achieved by asking profligate spenders to change their ways with pedantic lessons about compound interest or moralizing about the true value of money. By grafting the new service onto existing behavior, however, IDEO designed an experience both reassuringly familiar and invitingly new. Before they knew it, BofA's customers were achieving results they never had before and possibly never thought they would.

## building an experience culture by making everyone a design thinker

Nowhere is the challenge of designing compelling experiences greater than in the hotel industry—and in perhaps no other industry are the stakes higher. Any traveler can recall heart-stopping moments when an attentive member of a hotel staff has turned a potential disaster into a great experience, and the reverse is probably true as well. Whereas Bank of America had only to create a onetime interface, great hotel chains rise or fall on delivering flawless service with flawless consistency. And like all experience brands, they rely on people to a great degree.

Four Seasons Hotels are famous for their quality of service as much as for the luxury of their properties. They are also recognized within the industry for having a staff-training system in which staff members learn how to anticipate the needs of their customers and build on the ideas of their colleagues—essential qualities, as we have seen, of design thinkers. In one program, which looks like an appealing perk but is actually a very shrewd investment, qualified employees, after just six months employment, are eligible to put themselves on the receiving end of the luxury hotel experience by staying at any Four Seasons property worldwide. Employees come back from these sojourns with a first-person appreciation of the meaning of hospitality, fired up to provide the best and most empathetic experience possible. Four Seasons knows that exceptional experience starts with its own people.

Creating an experience culture requires going beyond the generic to design experiences perceived as uniquely tailored to each customer. Unlike a manufactured product or a standardized service, an experience comes to life when it feels personalized and customized. Sometimes this feeling can be achieved through technology, in the way that Yahoo! allows people to customize their search pages. Most often it comes from the ability of experience providers to add something special or appropriate at just the right moment. This sense of timing is rarely the result of a corporate strategy developed by marketing executives working miles away and months or even years before. The design team back at home base may do a wonderful job of creating a great stage for the experience and may even create some useful scripts to help keep it moving along, but they cannot anticipate every opportunity. That is why the training program at Four Seasons includes improvisation rather than drilling the staff with canned scripts. A real experience culture is a culture of spontaneity.

This insight inspired Ritz-Carlton, a Marriott International subsidiary and sister brand of Marriott Hotels, to ask us to help it think about how to take the building of an experience culture to scale across all of the fifty luxury hotels in the Ritz portfolio. Would it be possible to extend this idea of personalized experience to every one of the properties without losing the personal touch and sacrificing their unique character? The key to creating an integrated, coordinated experience, of course, was to avoid trying to create an integrated, coordinated experience.

IDEO designers decided to develop a two-piece program called "Scenography," intended to equip general managers with the tools to anticipate the needs and meet the expectations of their guests. In the first phase, they created a tool kit consisting of inspirational examples to show what a great experience culture might look like. Using visual language inspired by art and theater—scenes, props, mood—and original photography to capture a precise emotional ambience, they recast the hotelier not as operational manager but as artistic director, creatively empowered to choreograph a unique experience.

The second phase of "Scenography" addressed the fact that each hotel operates as an independent fiefdom full of local touches and property-specific management. Rather than propose a blandly uniform corporate identity across each of them, "Scenography" developed a template to help managers judge for themselves whether or not they were meeting the high standards sketched out in the imagined scenarios and even to craft their own scenes from scratch. The hospitality industry has a record of providing discrete products and isolated amenities. We wanted them to think about service as something that happens continuously over time, with many encounters and a strong emotional outcome. We were asking them, in effect, to tell a story through an experience.

What we learn from the hospitality industry, where brands are built on the delivery of great experiences, is that transforming the culture of an organization is every bit as important as designing the lobby or the curbside service. Empowering employees to seize opportunities when and where they see them and giving them the tools to create unscripted experiences is an essential element of that transformation. Rather than delivering a set of instructions created for them by a bunch of designers somewhere, we encourage them to become design thinkers themselves.

## executing the idea

On a recent trip to Grand Rapids, Michigan, my colleagues and I arrived in the early evening at a new JW Marriott hotel. Expecting to grab something to eat in town, we were instead met by one of our partners from Steelcase, who informed us that arrangements had been made for us to eat in the hotel's "stateroom." Images of the captain's table on the *Titanic* flashed through my mind. I began to feign symptoms of jet lag, but to no avail. We were escorted into the restaurant and then ushered through the serving doors into the kitchen, where we were greeted by sous chefs, pastry chefs, and waiters and led, finally, into the private office of the executive chef, where a table had been laid for us. We were deep in the inner sanctum, his private domain, surrounded by cookbooks, open wine bottles, favorite music, and all the clutter of a large-scale culinary operation. A perfect meal followed. We chatted with the chef about local produce, secrets of the kitchen, and tricks of the trade. I learned a lot about food that evening, but even more about design.

One does not have to be the executive chef of a fancy restaurant to realize that eating is about more than food, nutrition, or diet. When friends come to your house for dinner, you give plenty of thought to the experience: What will you cook? Should we eat indoors or out? Will the seating favor a subdued conversation with old friends, or should it be designed to impress a business associate or put a foreign visitor at ease? Thinking through this process is the difference between cooking a meal and designing an experience, but it's important not to get lost in the staging of the event: the effect will be lost if the salad is wilted, the chicken tastes like rubber, and you can't find the corkscrew. For an idea to become an experience, it must be implemented with the same care in which it is conceived.

A one-off experience such as a dinner party is a bit like a piece of fine woodworking: it works with the grain and bears the mark of the craftsman, and imperfections are part of its charm. When the experience is repeated many times, however, each of these elements must be precision-engineered to deliver the desired experience consistently and reliably. We can think of service design as equivalent to everything that goes into a great product such as a BMW. The designers and engineers go to great lengths to make sure the smell of the interior, the feel of the seats, the sound of the engine, and the look of the body all support and reinforce one another.

In designing houses, Frank Lloyd Wright was famous for the fastidiousness with which he attended to every aspect of the owner's experience. The Meyer May House, a modest residence in a suburban neighborhood in Grand Rapids, was designed to protect the privacy of owners and guests through the overall layout of the building, and detail after detail supports this overall objective. The dining room table is situated so that every person can see outside. The lighting is removed from the ceiling and placed on columns at each corner of the table to soften the light on each person's face. The chairs, designed with high backs, create an intimate border around the gathering. Wright also demanded that no high centerpieces be placed on the table to obscure the view between diners. Throughout the house, he designed the living experience down to the last detail.

Too much so, for many of Wright's critics and even some of his clients; the archives bulge with plaintive letters in which they humbly request permission to replace a piece of furniture or alter a window covering. When the wealthy industrialist Hibbard Johnson telephoned Wright to complain that the roof of his house had sprung a leak and rainwater was dripping on his head, the Master is said to have retorted, "Why don't you move your chair?" As tyrannical as he may have been, however (it has been said that he did not have clients so much as patrons), Wright was motivated by the belief that design and execution must work together if the architect is to deliver not just the house but the experience of it.

## the experience blueprint

In the days before large-format photocopy machines, never mind computer-aided design, technical drawings still needed to be reproduced for building contractors and workers on the factory floor. They used a chemical process that produced blue-lined prints with a strong smell of ammonia, and the "blueprint" became synonymous with the specifications used in manufacturing or construction. The blueprint reveals on a single page both the general plan and the specific detail, the final objective and the practical means of implementation. Just as a product begins with an engineering blueprint and a building with an architectural blueprint, an *experience blueprint* provides the framework for working out the details of a human interaction—without the smell of ammonia.

The difference is that unlike the plans for an office building or a table lamp, an experience blueprint also describes the *emotive* elements. It captures how people travel through an experience in time. Rather than trying to choreograph that journey, however, its function is to identify the most meaningful points and turn them into opportunities. The concept of an experiential blueprint emerged when Marriott decided to focus on the first, and presumably the most important, point of contact between the customer and the hotel: the experience of checking in.

Marriott had invested millions of dollars in enhancing what was assumed to be the critical moment in the customer journey. Architects were summoned. Operations manuals were prepared. Advertising agencies were put to work. There was only one problem with this strategy, however: the premise was based on assumptions, not observation. Marriott strategy assumed that when a weary traveler met a friendly face at the check-in counter, an interaction occurred that would color the remainder of the guest's visit. A closer look at the entirety of the picture revealed that even the best check-in experience was more akin to vaulting the final hurdle than to crossing the finish line.

To test this premise, a design team met travelers as they disembarked from their airplanes, accompanied them to the hotel in their taxis or rental cars, observed every detail of the check-in process, and then followed them up to their rooms. The genuinely important moment, they discovered, comes when the traveler enters his room, throws his coat onto the bed, turns on the television, and *exhales*. The "exhale moment," as it came to be called, presented the clearest opportunity for innovation and Marriott was persuaded to shift its resources in that direction.

As with an engineering or architectural blueprint, the experience blueprint takes the form of a physical document that guides the building of an experience. Unlike a prepared script or an operations manual, it connects the customer experience and the business opportunity. Every detail holds the potential to sour a relationship—confusing signage, an inattentive doorman—but only a few offer possibilities for an experience that is distinctive, emotionally gratifying, and memorable. The blueprint is at one and the same time a high-level strategy document and a fine-grained analysis of the details that matter.

From airlines and hospitals to supermarkets, banks, and hotels, it's clear that experiences are much more complex than inert objects. They vary from place to place, they change over time, and they are hard to get right. Although the design of an experience may involve products, services, spaces, and technology, an experience carries us beyond the comfortable world of measurable utility and into the hazy zone of emotional value.

The best and most successful experience brands have a number of things in common that may provide us with some secure guidelines. First, a successful experience requires active consumer participation. Second, a customer experience that feels authentic, genuine, and compelling is likely to be delivered by employees operating within an experience culture themselves. Third, every touchpoint must be executed with thoughtfulness and precision—experiences should be designed and engineered with the same attention to detail as a German car or a Swiss watch.

# spreading the message,
## or *the importance of storytelling*

I t's not so easy to get the prime minister of a G8 country to become part of your corporate marketing strategy, but Makoto Kakoi and Naoki Ito, senior account executives at the award-winning Japanese advertising agency Hakuhodo, used the power of storytelling to do exactly that in their brilliant Cool Biz campaign.

In 2005 the Ministry of the Environment, under the leadership of the imaginative minister Yuriko Koike, approached Hakuhodo for help in getting the Japanese people more involved in meeting Japan's commitment to the greenhouse gas reduction goals of the Kyoto Protocol. The government had made several previous attempts, but they had met with limited success. Hakuhodo suggested creating a campaign that mobilized the collectivist ethos of Japanese society toward a concrete goal: working together to reduce emissions by 6 percent. Within a year, according to a survey commissioned by the Ministry of the Environment, the slogan "Cool Biz" was recognized by a staggering 95.8 percent of the Japanese population.

The real challenge, as the Hakuhodo team recognized, was to make the campaign not only familiar but also meaningful. In pursuit of this elusive goal, they enlisted a group of experts to help them identify four hundred everyday activities that cause or reduce carbon emissions. This list was whittled down to six key practices, which included raising the thermostats on air-conditioning systems in summer and lowering them in winter; conserving water by turning off taps; driving less aggressively; selecting more ecofriendly products at the grocery store; ending the use of plastic bags; and turning off electronic products when not in use. Each of these activities was selected to create a balance of engagement and impact. They were activities that most people could integrate into their daily lives but that, cumulatively and over time, would make an enormous difference.

The target during the first year of the program was the air-conditioning problem. Conventionally these systems were set to 26 degrees C. (79 degrees F.) so that businessmen in their suits and ties could work comfortably in the hot, steamy Japanese summer, while female office workers in their short formal business skirts often covered their laps with blankets to stay warm. This oddity would have been bad enough if not for the inconvenient truth that cooling buildings to such a low temperature requires huge amounts of energy, especially during the summer months.

Hakuhodo created Cool Biz, a period from June 1 to October 1 every year when businessmen and women may wear more casual clothing, so that it is easier to stay cool. Air-conditioning thermostats could then be raised to 28 degrees C. (82 degrees F.) instead of 26, a small adjustment but one that created enormous energy savings. Ingrained cultural practice threatened to derail this sensible idea: how to get conservative Japanese businessmen to change the way they dress? Rather than bombarding people with a campaign of print and TV advertisements, the Hakuhodo team set up a Cool Biz fashion show at the Expo 2005 World Exposition in Aichi in which dozens of CEOs and other senior executives strutted about in casual business wear with open necks and lightweight materials. Even Prime Minister Junichiro Koizumi was featured in newspaper and TV stories tieless and in a short-sleeved shirt.

The event caused a sensation. In this traditional and hierarchical society, in which people defer to the guys at the top, a message went out that it was okay to depart from convention—business dress, in this case—to protect the environment. To help reinforce the message, the government distributed Cool Biz pins to any organization that signed on. It was forbidden to criticize coworkers for wearing casual clothing if they were wearing a Cool Biz badge. For the second time in a hundred years, the Japanese set about literally to reengineer their business etiquette. Within three years, 25,000 businesses throughout the country had signed on to Cool Biz and 2.5 million individuals had made commitments on the campaign's Web site. In Japan Cool Biz has now thawed to become Warm Biz to help save energy during the winter months, and Cool Biz sites have begun popping up in China, Korea, and elsewhere in Asia.

With Cool Biz, Hakuhodo turned an idea into a campaign and a campaign into a movement engaging millions of ordinary citizens and the political and business elite. Rather than relying on traditional advertising, Hakuhodo generated a conversation. Newspapers and magazines reported on the phenomenon because people wanted to know about it. The prime-time news media followed suit. Cool Biz had become a cool story.

Many notions have been proposed to explain what differentiates human beings from other species: bipedal locomotion, tool use, language, symbolic systems. Our ability to tell stories also sets us apart. In his provocative book *Nonzero*, the journalist Robert Wright makes the case that consciousness, language, and society have developed an intimate relationship with technologies of storytelling throughout the forty-thousand-year history of human society. As we learned how to spread our ideas, our social structures expanded from nomadic groups to tribes to settled villages and then to cities and states, followed by supranational organizations and movements. Before long the Japanese were cooling their buildings in the summer and heating them in the winter to make it bearable to go to work wearing Western-style clothes—and telling themselves stories about it.

Mostly we rely on stories to put our ideas into context and give them meaning. It should be no surprise, then, that the human capacity for storytelling plays an important role in the intrinsically human-centered approach to problem solving, *design thinking*.

## designing in the fourth dimension

We have already seen hints of storytelling at work: in ethnographic fieldwork; in the synthesis phase, in which we begin to make sense of large accumulations of data; and in the design of experiences. In each case, we are talking about adding not just a new widget but a whole new dimension to the designer's tool kit: the "fourth dimension," designing with time. When we create multiple touchpoints along a customer journey, we are structuring a sequence of events that build upon one another, in sequential order, across time. Storyboards, improvisation, and scenarios are among the many narrative techniques that help us visualize an idea as it unfolds over time.

Designing with time is a little different from designing in space. The design thinker has to be comfortable moving along both of these axes. I learned this back in the mid-1980s, when designers working in the computer industry were still concerned mostly with hardware (remember all those beige boxes?). Software was still the domain of geeks in computer labs, not designers, much less students in classrooms, workers in offices, or consumers at home. The Apple Macintosh, which was oriented toward a mass market, changed everything. The smiley Mac icon told a completely different story from the blinking green cursor of MS-DOS.

The talented designers at the core of the Macintosh software team—Bill Atkinson, Larry Tesler, Andy Hertzfeld, Susan Kare—were by no means the only ones thinking about how to create a seamless computing experience at that time. In 1981 Bill Moggridge, having been lured from Britain to the Bay Area by the challenges of the emerging digital technology, began work on the design of a curious little "laptop" computer for a Silicon Valley start-up called GRiD Systems. The team received a patent for the idea of folding a thin, flat screen down over the keyboard. The GRiD Compass established the standard layout for the laptop computer and went on to win countless awards. Once the computer was turned on, however, the terrible DOS-based operating system overwhelmed the experience. To perform the simplest operation, it was necessary to type an arcane sequence of commands that bore no relation to lived experience—in the sharpest contrast to the ingenious device, which folded in half like a notebook and disappeared into a briefcase.

Inspired by the Mac and the GRiD, Moggridge decided there had to be a role for professional designers in software development—the insides, as it were, and not just the outsides of computers. This led him to propose a new discipline: interaction design. In 1988, when I joined Bill's team at ID Two in San Francisco, I worked with a small team of interaction designers on projects for computer-aided design, network management, and later video games and various online entertainment systems. For an industrial designer accustomed to designing discrete physical objects, designing for a series of dynamic interactions over time was transformative. I realized I had to have a deeper understanding of the people for whom I was designing. I had to think as much about their actions as the objects they were using—"We are designing verbs," Moggridge kept reminding us, "not nouns."

To design an interaction is to allow a story to unfold over time. This realization has led interaction designers to experiment with the use of narrative techniques such as storyboards and scenarios borrowed from other fields of design. When working on the predecessor of the modern GPS system for Trimble Navigation, for instance, the designers told a story about how a sailor might navigate from one port to the next. Each scene described some important step that would have to be designed into the system. In the early days interaction designers tended to be too prescriptive. Today, they are learning to let go and to allow the user a greater say in determining how things unfold. Almost everything now has an interactive component. The distinction between software and the products in which it is embedded has blurred, and time-based narrative techniques have entered into every field of design.

# taking time to design

One of the many problems bedeviling the health care system to-day is "adherence." Once a doctor has diagnosed a condition, pa-tients often fail to take the prescribed medicine for the duration of the therapy. The pharmaceutical industry is concerned about this for its own reasons: drug companies lose billions of dollars each year because patients give up on their medications. But ad-herence is a serious medical issue as well. In the phrase of the incurably blunt former Surgeon General C. Edward Koop, "Pills don't work if people don't take them!" In the case of chronic con-ditions such as heart disease or high blood pressure, patients risk letting the condition get worse. In other situations—antibiotic treatments of bacterial infections, for instance—they may put others at risk by releasing attenuated drug-resistant microorgan-isms back into the larger population.

IDEO has worked with several pharmaceutical companies on specific drug adherence regimes. The brief: drug companies spend hundreds of millions of dollars, often using aggressive mar-keting techniques, to promote their drugs, only to lose much of the therapeutic, and business, advantage when the patient stops taking them. They are taking a traditional approach to selling a product rather than creating an experience that engages the patient over time. Rather than badgering doctors with unwanted sales visits and the public with obnoxious television commercials, pharmaceutical companies should use design thinking to explore a new approach to the business of pills.

There are three self-reinforcing phases of medical treatment. First, the patient must understand his or her condition, then accept the need for treatment, and finally take action. This time-based "adherence loop" suggests a framework with many different points at which it is possible to provide patients with needed positive reinforcement. We can design better information to educate people about their disease; there could be better methods for dispensing and administering medications; along the "adherence journey" the patient might find support groups, Web sites, and call centers staffed by nurses. The specific set of tools will vary according to the particular disease or treatment, but two underlying principles are the same: first, as with every other type of time-based design project, each patient's journey through the process will be unique; second, it will be far more effective to engage individuals as active participants in their own stories. Designing with time means thinking of people as living, growing, thinking organisms who can help write their own stories.

## the politics of new ideas

An experience that unfolds over time, engages participants, and allows them to tell their own stories will have resolved two of the biggest obstacles in the path of every new idea: gaining acceptance in one's own organization and getting it out into the world. An idea may be a product, service, or strategy.

More good ideas die because they fail to navigate the treacherous waters of the organization where they originate than because the market rejects them. Any complex organization must balance numerous competing interests, and new ideas, as Harvard's Clayton Christensen argues, are disruptive. If it is truly innovative, it challenges the status quo. Such innovations often threaten to cannibalize previous successes and recast yesterday's innovators as today's conservatives. They take resources away from other important programs. They make life harder for managers by presenting them with new choices, each with unknown risks—including the risk of making no choice at all. Considering all of these potential obstacles, it is a wonder that new ideas make it through large organizations at all.

At the heart of any good story is a central narrative about the way an idea satisfies a need in some powerful way: coordinating a dinner date with friends on opposite sides of town; making a discreet insulin injection during a business meeting; converting from a gasoline-powered to an electric-powered car. As it unfolds, the story will give every character represented in it a sense of purpose and will unfold in a way that involves every participant in the action. It will be convincing but not overwhelm us with unnecessary detail. It will include plenty of detail to ground it to some plausible reality. It will leave the audience with no doubt that the organization "narrating" it has what it takes to make it real. All this takes skill and imagination, as a group of executives from Snap-on discovered.

From the neighborhood gas station to the vast maintenance terminals of the major commercial airlines, the bright-red-and-silver Snap-on toolbox is an icon of machine shops everywhere. The Wisconsin-based company felt less certain about how to tell a compelling story about the computerized products that were the key to its future survival. Every garage mechanic feels an emotional connection with his hand tools, but it's not so easy to personalize the experience of an electronic diagnostic device that interrogates a car's onboard computer to identify problems and parts in need of repair. Where Snap-on saw a problem, a design team at IDEO saw an opportunity to tell a new story.

Once the brief was settled, the team took over an abandoned automobile-repair shop a couple of blocks away in Palo Alto. During a frenetic week of activity, they transformed the place into a space-time narrative their client would not soon forget. On the day of the final presentation, the Snap-on visitors headed up the street to the garage, in front of which was parked a fleet of Ferraris, Porsches, and BMWs, all in the signature Snap-on colors of silver and red.

After a wine-and-cheese greeting, the executives were given a briefing in the main garage bay, then ushered into a room with a museumlike display of inspirational artifacts, and finally to a screening of videos of real mechanics talking about the Snap-on brand. The story reached its climax when the Snap-on executives were led from the makeshift theater into a darkened room. As the lights faded up, they found themselves surrounded by sleek prototypes of a new generation of diagnostic devices transformed from generic computers to high-tech siblings of Snap-on's iconic wrenches and toolboxes. Posters advertising products based on the new brand strategy lined the walls. As the CEO and president played with the models, the marketing VP sponsoring the project stood by with tears streaming down her cheeks. Though it's not always necessary to make your audience cry, a good story well told should deliver a powerful emotional punch.

## when the point of the story is the story

Design thinking can help bring new products to the world, but there are occasions when it is the story itself that is the final product—when the point is to introduce what the evolutionary biologist Richard Dawkins famously called a "meme," a self-propagating idea that changes behavior, perceptions, or attitudes. In today's noisy business environment, where top-down authority has become suspect and centralized administration is no longer sufficient, a transformative idea needs to diffuse on its own. If your employees or customers don't understand where you are going, they will not be able to help you get there. This is doubly true in the case of technology companies and other businesses whose product may not be easily recognized or understood.

Chip designers live in the back room of the computing industry. Nothing would work without them, but no matter how vital their contribution, it is hard to build a brand around a microscopic chip that sits on a board that sits inside a device that sits inside a box. This is the genius of the little "intel inside" sticker affixed to so many of the world's PCs. In the highly competitive computer industry, where Moore's Law humbles the mighty and technological advantages are short-lived, Intel has built a powerful global brand that is meaningful to consumers even though they cannot see it or hold it in their hands.

More recently, pursuing what the Stanford professor of organizational behavior Chip Heath calls "ideas that stick," Intel has moved from adhesive labels to an approach that uses storytelling to explore the future of computing. Having conquered the desktop, Intel is now promoting a shift to mobile computing. Oftentimes these projects are showcased at influential industry events such as the Intel Developer Forum, but it can be hard to demo a product that hasn't been created yet. It's easier just to sit back and enjoy a movie.

Most of us are already lugging around "laptop" computers in our briefcases and backpacks, but Intel wanted to show what life might be like in a world of ultramobile computing—the next generation of smart phones and other devices we might carry with us all the time. Using sophisticated computer graphics, a design team working with Intel created "Future Vision," a series of film scenarios intended to show how we might in the near future integrate mobile computing into our daily rhythms: a Mandarin-speaking businessman finds his way to the offices of his American partner while preparing for a tough negotiating session; a jogger receives a Wi-Fi notification that his afternoon meeting has been moved forward to 8:30 a.m.; shoppers compare prices; and friends coordinate their urban movements in real time. The design team even arranged for "Future Vision" to be uploaded onto YouTube, where it has been seen by well over half a million people.

Intel did not have to go to Hollywood to make "Future Vision." A design team, working with a talented film crew, completed the entire project in a few weeks and at a fraction of the cost of a conventional ad. Effective storytelling, even with high production value, does not have to break the bank.

## propagating the faith

Should an idea manage to survive the perilous journey through an organization and out into the market, storytelling can play another vital if obvious role: communicating its value to its intended audience in such a way that some of them, at least, want to go out and buy it.

We are all familiar with the power of great advertising to tell stories, and create myths, about new products. I remember as a kid in the United Kingdom in the 1970s watching the great TV "adverts" for Hamlet cigars, Silk Cut cigarettes, and Cadbury's Smash. They were clever, funny, and engaging. Advertising, in those days, greased the wheels of the consumer economy, and it resonated with a more optimistic, less skeptical public. By then, however, there were already indications that things were changing: I loved the ads, but I never took up smoking and the taste of the powdered potato mix that went into Cadbury's Smash still makes me slightly nauseous.

Many observers have commented on the decline in the effectiveness of traditional advertising. One simple reason is that fewer people are reading, looking at, or listening to traditional forms of broadcast media. But there are other reasons why thirty-second spots no longer serve as an effective vehicle for new ideas, including what the Swarthmore College psychologist Barry Schwartz has identified as "the paradox of choice." Most people don't want more options; they just want what they want. When overwhelmed by choice, we tend to fall into behavioral patterns used by those whom Schwartz calls "optimizers"— people paralyzed by the fear that if they only waited a little while longer or searched a little harder, they could find what they think they want at the best possible price. That was not a problem in the days when "automobile" meant a black Model T or "the phone company" meant AT&T. The other camp is populated by "satisficers," who have given up on making consumer decisions and will put up with whatever works. Neither presents marketing departments with a happy situation, and marketers have been driven to increasingly desperate measures to deal with the fact, with dubious results. I suspect that I am not the only one who can recall an ad but have no idea which financial service, pain reliever, or limited-time offer it advertised.

From the perspective of the design thinker, a new idea will have to tell a meaningful story in a compelling way if it is to make itself heard. There is still a role for advertising, but less as a medium for blasting messages at people than as a way of helping turn its audience into storytellers themselves. Anyone who has a positive experience with an idea should be able to communicate its essential elements in a way that encourages other people to try it out for themselves. Bank of America launched its successful Keep the Change offering with plenty of advertising, but the campaign served mostly to build on a habit many customers already practiced and make them propagandists for it.

Examples abound of effective storytelling, of design thinking engaging an audience and playing itself out in the medium of time. When the MINI Cooper brand launched in the USA, BMW made excellent use of storytelling to market a brand. Instead of relying on the normal mind-numbing TV ads full of cars speeding through the mountains or depositing their elegantly dressed cargo in front of fancy restaurants, the creative agency Crispin Porter + Bogusky exploited the car's small, cute, and irreverent character. Their "Let's motor!" campaign evoked the story of David and Goliath, with the diminutive MINI bravely arrayed against its gigantic American competitors. MINI billboard ads appeared everywhere, and their clever visual puns inspired spontaneous storytelling about the place of the MINI—and of the billboards advertising it!—in the urban environment. Magazine pullouts included fold-up MINIs. In one particularly nasty tweak to the U.S. auto industry, professional drivers tooled around Manhattan in SUVs with MINIs strapped to the roof! After signing the papers—including one headed "The Sucky Financial Bit"—new buyers were given a personal Web site where they could follow the progress of their MINI being made. All of these clever marketing tools not only were well executed, they also got people talking, and that became part of the story.

## the challenge of a good challenge

There is almost no trick in the design thinker's tool kit more enjoyable to observe or more productive of results than a "design challenge." This exercise takes the form of a structured competition in which rival teams attack a single problem. A single team usually comes out on top, but the collective energy and intelligence they mobilize ensures that everybody wins. IDEO was recently asked by one of the Bay Area's leading art schools to help imagine the future of the institution, so we spent most of the modest budget hiring the school's own design students to figure it out in rival teams; the results exceeded everyone's expectations.

The creative team at Hakuhodo, the Japanese advertising firm that created the Cool Biz campaign, experimented with another twist on the design challenge. The battery division of Panasonic had been struggling with its Oxyride battery, which is more powerful and longer lasting than a normal alkaline battery but is otherwise indistinguishable from its countless competitors. Rather than running a normal ad campaign promoting Oxyride's technology, the Hakuhodo team posed a simple question: "Can man fly on the power of household batteries alone?"

For four months a group of student engineers from the Tokyo Institute of Technology worked on the design and construction of a battery-powered, piloted airplane, while a TV show followed their progress and a Web site stoked public curiosity and built support for the team. At 6:45 on the morning of July 16, 2006, three hundred journalists turned up to watch as the plane took off from a makeshift runway and soared almost 400 meters (1,300 feet)—powered by 160 Oxyride AA batteries. All the Japanese news channels covered the flight, and the story found its way into international news services, including the BBC and *Time.* The event generated media coverage that Panasonic estimated to be worth at least $4 million, and Oxyride's brand recognition jumped by 30 percent. Hakuhodo and Panasonic used a simple design challenge to turn advertising on its head. The aircraft even ended up in the National Science Museum—an honor not shared by the Energizer Bunny!

A decade before the first battery-powered manned flight, the spaceflight activist Dr. Peter Diamandis used a dramatic design challenge to capture the public imagination and stimulate a major technological initiative. According to the terms of the first Ansari X Prize, announced in 1996, a nongovernmental team must build and launch a spacecraft capable of carrying three people to an altitude of 100 kilometers (62 miles) above the earth's surface and repeat the feat within two weeks. The challenge was a huge success. Twenty-six teams from seven countries spent more than $100 million before SpaceShipOne, the team from Burt Rutan's company, Scaled Composites, won the prize on October 4, 2004. Since then, and in large measure due to the X Prize challenge, entrepreneurs have invested more than $1.5 billion in support of the private spaceflight industry. The X Prize Foundation has extended its program of "Revolution Through Competition" to superefficient cars, genomics, and landing robots on the moon. Numerous other organizations have followed Diamandis's example.

Design challenges are not only a great way to unleash the power of competition, they also create stories around an idea, transforming people from passive onlookers into engaged participants. People love the idea of following bands of adventurers as they compete to achieve the impossible. Reality TV has exploited this fascination with dubious results, but organizations such as the X Prize Foundation have shown how this same fascination can be mobilized to fulfill technological dreams and achieve profound humanitarian goals.

## from chasing numbers to serving humans

Effective storytelling, as part of a larger campaign of using the element of time to advance an integrated program of design thinking, relies on two critical moments: the beginning and the end. At the front end, it is essential that storytelling begin early in the life of a project and be woven into every aspect of the innovation effort. It has been common practice for design teams to bring writers in at the end to document a project once it has been completed. Increasingly they are building them into the design team from day one to help move the story along in real time. At the far end, a story gains traction when it is picked up by its intended audience, who feel motivated to carry it forward long after the design team has disbanded and moved on to other projects.

Among the many ways that the American Red Cross provides relief to the disadvantaged, one of the most important is large-scale donor blood collection. This volunteer-run organization goes to schools and workplaces and sets up a donor clinic for a day. In recent years the donor base has been shrinking, however, and the Red Cross decided to apply design thinking to the challenge of increasing the percentage of Americans donating blood from 3 percent of the population to 4 percent. This meant shifting the question from percentage points to a more human-centered focus: What are the emotional factors that lead people to donate blood or refrain from doing so? How might we improve the donor experience to make more people want to give blood?

Together, the IDEO–Red Cross team explored various ways of making the temporary field clinics more comfortable for the donor and easier for the all-volunteer staff to set up and take down. Numerous practical ideas resulted from the effort—storage units that doubled as furniture, a system of mobile carts—but one detail expressed the new, human-centered orientation: in the course of repeated on-site observations, the design team noted that many people had strong personal motivations for giving blood—in memory of a lost family member or on behalf of a close friend whose life had been saved by a blood donation. The stories they told were powerful and often the reason why donors came back again and again and even recruited their friends and coworkers.

The design team decided that better signage and more comfortable seating were less important than inviting people to share their stories and thus reinforce the emotional reasons for giving blood. Returning donors might feel that their private experiences were connected to something larger. New donors might learn something about the range of motivations behind this altruistic act. In the new experience, when donors check in they are given a card and invited to write a brief story about their reasons for wanting to give blood. Donors who wish to have their pictures taken can add their photograph to the card before it is posted on a board in the waiting area. What could be simpler than telling a story and sharing it with others, each of whom is there for a different reason but who are bound to one another by a common commitment?

On the basis of promising results from a prototype set up in North Carolina, the American Red Cross is preparing to move forward with full-scale pilot programs in Minnesota and Connecticut.

## life after the thirty-second spot

The sheer excess characteristic of our time—of goods, services, and information—is one reason for the declining success of conventional advertising. A second reason is that we ourselves are growing more complex and sophisticated. With access to greater volumes of information than could have been imagined by our parents' generation, our judgments are more complex and our choices more discerning. One need only look at the hopelessly dated jingles and antics that enlivened the commercials of our childhoods to see how far we have come. It's become impossible to sell a box of laundry detergent—much less communicate the urgency of an idea such as global warming—through a thirty-second spot.

As a result, storytelling needs to be in the tool kit of the design thinker—in the sense not of a tidy beginning, middle, and end but of an ongoing, open-ended narrative that engages people and encourages them to carry it forward and write their own conclusions. Herein lies the success of the forceful story created by Al Gore and told in his Academy Award–winning movie, *An Inconvenient Truth*. By the end of the film the Nobel laureate, Academy Award winner, and self-described "former next president of the United States" presents the evidence of global warming to his viewers and challenges them to make it their own.

"Design" is no longer a discrete stylistic gesture thrown at a project just before it is handed off to marketing. The new approach taking shape in companies and organizations around the world moves design backward to the earliest stages of a product's conception and forward to the last stages of its implementation—and beyond. Allowing customers to write the last chapter of the story themselves is only one more example of design thinking in action.

In each of the preceding chapters I have tried to identify techniques that originated in the design community—field observations, prototyping, visual storytelling—that lie at the center of a human-centered design process. In the course of these studies I have made two arguments: First, that it is time for these skills to migrate outward into all parts of organizations and upward into the highest levels of leadership. Design thinking can be practiced by everybody. There is no reason why everyone, up to and including the "C-level"—CEOs, CFOs, CTOs, and COOs—cannot master these thought processes as well.

The second part of my argument will become clearer in the chapters that make up part two. It is that as design thinking begins to move out of the studio and into the corporation, the service sector, and the public sphere, it can help us to grapple with a vastly greater range of problems than has previously been the case. Design can help to improve our lives in the present. Design thinking can help us chart a path into the future.

# PART II

## where do we go from here?

In the first part of this book we saw how business leaders, hospital administrators, university professors, and NGOs have begun to integrate the methods of the designer and, conversely, how designers have broadened their reach from the crafting of objects to the shaping of services, experiences, and organizations. Part two begins by looking at some case studies of what happens when the various elements of the design thinking methodology come together in an integrated, coordinated strategy.

I then turn to what comes next: how can we apply this framework to the problems facing business and society today? We are at a critical point where rapid change is forcing us to look not just to new ways of solving problems but to new problems to solve.

# design thinking meets the corporation,

## or *teaching to fish*

S ince the early 1990s, Nokia has been the most consistently successful cell phone manufacturer in the world. Its products dominate markets from Munich to Mumbai and from Montreal to Mexico City. Nokia began as a paper mill in 1865 and through a sequence of investments moved from paper to rubber, cables, electronics, and ultimately mobile phones. A combination of technological prowess, organizational innovation, and top-notch industrial design kept Nokia ahead of the pack. In the last few years, however, the emergence of the mobile Internet has changed the rules of the game. In a growing number of markets it is no longer enough to have a snappy device with which to make a phone call or send a text. People want mobile information services, whether for searching maps or for networking with friends. Indeed, many customers in emerging countries will have their first Internet experience not on a PC but through a mobile handset. It is no longer the hardware that matters but the services and applications it delivers.

Nokia saw this coming and in 2006 began to explore alternatives to its existing hardware-driven approach. Technologists, anthropologists, and designers were sent out into the world to understand how consumers were communicating, sharing information, and entertaining themselves and to look for what was missing. They found that people no longer simply wanted to make telephone calls. They wanted to express their creativity, to discover new things, and to share what they found with others. They also found that people were often forced to cobble together a variety of devices to make this happen. Nokia had all the components—three-megapixel cameras with high-quality Zeiss lenses, 3G and Wi-Fi network connectivity—but they were not integrated with services that could connect people in richer, more powerful ways.

On the basis of these observations Nokia's design teams brainstormed, prototyped, and explored a variety of new ideas that would enable the company to meet this need and seize this opportunity: mobile blogging, online gaming, photo sharing, location services, and time management. The teams presented these concepts to management in the form of stories from the field and future-oriented scenarios intended to show how these new services might be pulled together into a seamless experience that involved not just the phone but the Web and desktop.

Under the new model, Nokia would continue to design and sell mobile handsets, but the design teams were proposing a radical new future in which hardware ceased to be the company's offering and became the platform for a richly interactive, service-based business. Barely a year later, Nokia announced Ovi, a new service offering that could be accessed through any of its multimedia devices. Design thinking had enabled Nokia not only to explore new possibilities but also to convince itself that these possibilities were sufficiently compelling to move away from its strongly entrenched and previously successful approach. The timing was right. Today Ovi is one of the operating business divisions of the company, and Nokia—a technology leader—has reinvented itself as a service provider.

The rethinking of Nokia's business strategy did not come out of nowhere. To the contrary, its origins lie in a sweeping reassessment of the role of technology that has been under way since the end of World War II.

## design thinking as a systematic approach to innovation

In 1940, during the darkest hours of the Battle of Britain, the celebrated film director Humphrey Jennings rallied the nation with an inspiring newsreel documentary entitled "London Can Take It!" Six years later the war was over and democracy had prevailed. As Great Britain's battered economy struggled to recover, the Council of Industrial Design rose to rally the nation, this time with an ambitious exhibition called "Britain Can Make It." The sprawling exhibition, which covered 90,000 square feet at the Victoria and Albert Museum, foreshadowed how developed nations would take advantage of wartime breakthroughs in everything from electronics to ergonomics to revive consumer demand.

The wartime emergency led to massive and unprecedented government investment. In the postwar era, the initiative passed to the private sector. R&D labs flourished in every industry—from agriculture to automobiles and from textiles to telecommunications—staffed with the graduates of the technical universities of the United States, Europe, and Japan. Major expositions such as the Festival of Britain of 1951 and the sequence of World's Fairs that followed reaffirmed the belief that science would answer all our questions and technology would translate them into goods to satisfy every need.

The steady growth of corporate R&D labs, from barely 25,000 employees in the United States in 1958 to more than 1 million today, was a striking feature of the business landscape during the postwar decades. Geographically concentrated centers of technical innovation began to emerge along Route 128 in Massachusetts, in Cambridge in England, in the suburbs of Tokyo, and ultimately in the most successful of them all, northern California's Silicon Valley. The first sector to show results was the manufacturing of consumer goods. Then came computer and communications hardware, software applications, and the Internet, each of which has taken on the mantle of driving economic growth. Research and development became the pathway to competitive success.

Increasingly, however—as the example of Nokia shows—large companies are finding that a sole reliance on technical prowess is less effective in today's market than it once was. Some of the great R&D labs, such as Xerox Corporation's Palo Alto Research Center (PARC) and Bell Labs have either disappeared altogether or lost the privileged status they once had. Many companies have shifted the horizon of their research programs from long-term basic research to shorter-term applied innovation.

This is not necessarily a bad thing. Small technology-driven companies and innovation-minded start-ups often have an advantage over larger, more established businesses. As the "desirability-feasibility-viability" triad suggests, a company that comes at innovation from the direction of technical feasibility will have to adjust the other factors in response to whatever discoveries it makes. The ultimate business model for a new company may not be obvious at the outset, and in such a case flexibility and adaptability are an enormous asset. Google discovered the power of connecting search to advertising only after it had been in business for a while. It was the fledgling Apple Computer, not the mighty Xerox Corporation, that was able to bring Xerox's own research into computer interfaces to the market in the form of the Mac desktop icons and the mouse.

Large companies are better positioned to look for breakthroughs from within their existing markets, where technical virtuosity provides no assurance of success. It may make better sense to drive innovation from a consumer-centered perspective that allows them to exploit assets they already possess: a large customer base, recognized and trusted brands, experienced customer service and support systems, wide distribution and supply chains. This is the human-centered, desirability-based approach that design thinking is ideally suited to enhance. It has helped established companies as diverse as Procter & Gamble, Nike, ConAgra, and Nokia avoid overrelying on technology and gambling on the big hit.

## using design thinking to manage an innovation portfolio

In an organization with its share of oddballs, IDEO's Diego Rodriguez and Ryan Jacoby stand out. Like most of their colleagues, Diego and Ryan have strong design credentials, but each of them also holds an MBA. For a long time we avoided hiring business school graduates—not because they weren't smart or might show up at brainstorms wearing suits but because we figured they would have a hard time adjusting to the divergent, synthesis-based methods design thinking demands. We have had to reconsider that idea.

For one thing, the MBA curriculum at many institutions now grapples with the theory and practice of innovation, and a growing number of their graduates are drawn to the kinds of problems designers address. There are even a few places—the Hasso Plattner Institute of Design at Stanford, the Haas School of Business at Berkeley, and the Rotman School of Management at the University of Toronto—where business school students work directly on design projects. And at least one institution— the California College of the Arts in San Francisco—is taking seriously Tom Peters's widely reported announcement that "the MFA is the new MBA" and offers an MBA in design strategy alongside its programs in painting, printmaking, and photography. There is now a critical mass of business school graduates whose training has prepared them for the unconventional practices of design thinking.

Second, business thinking is integral to design thinking. A design solution can only benefit from the sophisticated analytical tools—discovery-driven planning, option and portfolio theory, prospect theory, customer lifetime value—that have evolved in the business sector. The unforgiving world of business can help design teams think responsibly about constraints, even as designers test those constraints as a project moves along. In prototyping an e-banking concept, for instance, an interaction designer might observe that the assumed source of revenue, advertising, would compromise the quality of the user experience. A business-oriented designer on the team might respond by evaluating alternatives to advertising, such as subscriptions or referral fees. This collaborative process allows everyone to assess the "viability" component of the innovation equation in creative ways, not merely as an after-the-fact market analysis.

Alongside their ongoing project commitments, Diego and Ryan have applied their business expertise to thinking about how companies can manage their portfolios of design-based innovation. Based on their own case studies, they developed a tool they call the "Ways to Grow" matrix, which evaluates the innovation efforts within an organization. By mapping innovation efforts along a vertical axis representing existing to new offerings and a horizontal axis representing existing to new users, companies can get a good picture of the balance of their innovation efforts.

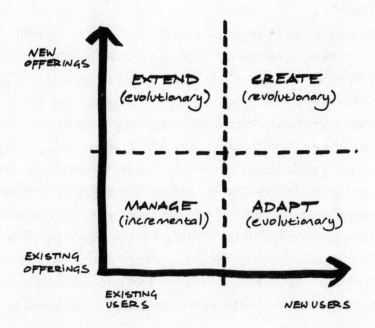

Projects in the bottom-left quadrant—close to existing offerings and existing users—tend to be incremental in nature.
They are important, and, indeed, the majority of a company's
effort is likely to be put into this type of innovation, which
might include the extension of a successful brand or the next
iteration of a current product. The aisles of any supermarket
provide countless examples of incremental innovation: each of
the dozens of flavors of toothpaste came from a process of incremental innovation and probably resulted in increased sales
for the manufacturer. In the auto industry, where the costs of
tooling can be astronomical, the vast majority of efforts are focused around incremental innovation—improvements to an existing model or the extension of an existing range. Auto manufacturers worldwide have suffered during the current recession,
but those that have focused only on incremental innovation,
namely Detroit's "Big Three," find themselves in the deepest
trouble of all.

In addition to incremental projects that secure a company's
base, it is vital to pursue evolutionary projects that stretch that
base in new directions. This more venturesome goal can be
reached either by *extending* existing offerings to solve the unmet needs of current customers or *adapting* them to meet the
needs of new customers or markets. The Prius is an example of
this type of evolutionary innovation. Through clever engineering and great design, Toyota captured the emerging demand
for energy-efficient personal transportation while its American
competitors were riding the existing wave of ever-larger SUVs.
With fortuitous timing, the Prius offered customers significantly lower fuel consumption just as fuel prices in the United
States leaped upward. The real innovation, however, was not

just the hybrid electric motor but the large, colorful information display that gives drivers a minute-by-minute indication of fuel economy, constantly challenging them to improve the fuel efficiency of their driving. Toyota is positioned to weather the economic storm because it invested in evolutionary, not just incremental, innovation.

Evolutionary innovation along the user axis might involve adapting an existing product so that it can be manufactured at a lower cost and thus marketed to a wider population. This is the concept underlying Tata Motors' controversial microcar, the Nano. The Nano is neither a new nor an original automobile; European microcars have been available since the 1950s. But a vehicle like Mercedes' $12,000 Smart car is still beyond the reach of much of the Indian market. Tata responded by engineering a car that has most of the features consumers expect but at a much lower cost. The Nano's two-cylinder engine is more compact and lighter in weight than any previous engine and is therefore cheaper to manufacture. Its electronic engine management system allows it to get fifty-four miles per gallon and to produce lower emissions than the millions of two-wheeled vehicles now sputtering along India's crowded roads. At a projected purchase price of just $2,000 the Nano is poised to reach a market previously inaccessible to car manufacturers.

The most challenging type of innovation—and the riskiest—is that in which both the product *and* the users are new. A revolutionary innovation *creates* entirely new markets, but this happens only rarely. Sony achieved this feat with the Walkman, and Apple did so twenty years later with its brilliant successor, the iPod. In neither case was the core technology new, but both companies succeeded in creating a market for a different type of musical experience. The Segway Personal Transporter, by contrast, is an instructive failure. The self-described "serial inventor" Dean Kamen identified a need for a means of urban transport in situations where distances are too long for walking but not long enough to justify getting into our cars. Using sophisticated gyroscopic technology, he invented a clever two-wheeled vehicle that automatically balances itself as it whisks travelers along the sidewalks of their towns and neighborhoods.

At first glance the Segway looks like a classic example of disruptive innovation. It provides a wholly new solution to a problem many people didn't know they had. However, instead of the spectacular success predicted by Segway's promoters, the results have been disappointing. At upward of $4,000 it would be easy to point to cost as the problem. I would point to the lack of a deep, human-centered analysis of how people might make the Segway part of their lives. It is enough to watch a brave early adopter dragging her Segway up the steps of her apartment building, to see a flock of tourists—already self-conscious—whizzing past the Eiffel Tower, or to hear how a postal worker cannot get enough life out of its lithium battery to complete his route to realize that invention is not the same as innovation. If a multidisciplinary design team had gone out into the field to understand the realities of urban life, conducted analogous observations, created scenarios and storyboards, brainstormed late into the night, built early prototypes of pipe cleaners and later ones using real users in real situations, and allowed its thinking to diverge before settling upon a single concept, we might all be cruising around town on our Segway Personal Transporters.

The "Ways to Grow" matrix is a tool of design thinking

that companies can use to manage their innovation portfolios and remain competitive in a constantly changing world. Although the imagination may be drawn to the once-in-a-lifetime smash hits, these are few and far between. And though it may be tempting to focus on incremental projects in which business forecasts are easy to make, this shortsighted approach leaves companies vulnerable to the unforeseeable events of the type that Nassim Nicholas Taleb dubbed the "Black Swan." Game-changing events may occur at any moment and will upend the most cautious business plan. Integrated digital music dethroned Sony. The whole of the conventional music-publishing industry was ill prepared for the disruptive impact of the Internet. The hushed auction chambers of Christie's and Sotheby's were no match for the raucous clamor of eBay. While there is no greater clarity than 20/20 hindsight, the financial meltdown of 2008 demonstrated that no company is "too big to fail" and even the most robust organizations would do well to write themselves an insurance policy. The next Black Swan could come from the labs of Genentech, the towers of Wall Street, or the caves of Tora Bora. A company's best defense is to diversify its portfolio by investing across all four quadrants of the innovation matrix.

## transforming organizations

Here, then, are the paired challenges facing most companies today: how to incorporate designers' creative problem-solving skills into their larger strategic initiatives and how to engage a far greater percentage of their workforce in design thinking itself. Designers have learned that it is possible to add doctors and nurses to their project teams, not to mention supermarket clerks, warehouse workers, office staff, professional athletes, marketing executives, HR managers, truck drivers, and union representatives. It is no less realistic to ask junior marketing executives and senior research scientists from the same organization to join forces and think beyond their respective disciplines. Some of the boldest initiatives in today's business landscape come from companies that are using design thinking to increase their innovation efforts and drive their growth.

When I speak to CEOs, the question they most often ask is "How can I make my company more innovative?" They recognize that in today's fluid business environment innovation is key to their competitiveness, but they are equally aware of the difficulties in focusing their organizations around this goal. Jim Hackett, the CEO of Steelcase, is one of a small number of enlightened business leaders who understand that a steady flow of innovative products rests upon an underlying *culture* of innovation. While he is excited by the challenge of designing new products, he is even more excited by the challenge of designing the organization itself.

Like many innovators, Hackett paid a price for coming to this question years before the business press turned "innovation" into a new kind of religion. There were no road maps to help him achieve his goals and few metrics to help gauge his success. Over time, however, through the hard work of his leadership team and his own willingness to experiment, Steelcase came to look like a different company from the one that offered the world its first fireproof wastebasket back in 1914. Whereas once technology and manufacturing capability drove most of its new-product development, the innovation process at Steelcase now begins with a focus on the needs of users and customers. Steelcase works outward from the perspective of human-centered design thinking.

One unit within the company, Workplace Futures, operates as a sort of internal think tank to explore areas ranging from higher education to information technology. Workplace Futures includes anthropologists, industrial designers, and business strategists who conduct observations in the field to gain insights into the problems of Steelcase's actual and potential clients. They develop scenarios to help them anticipate the future needs of university researchers, IT workers, or hotel managers; build prototypes to help them visualize solutions; and create compelling stories describing potential opportunities. Sales teams are then in a position to collaborate with customers to solve problems instead of simply trying to sell them the latest range of products.

Workplace Futures has identified health care as a particularly significant opportunity, and on the basis of its forecasts Steelcase has launched a fast-growing business called Nurture that specializes in health care environments. Nurture's teams have worked on projects that range from outfitting the brand-new, state-of-the-art Metro Health Hospital in Wyoming, Michigan, to prototyping a single room in the Sidney Hillman Health Center in New York City, a nonprofit facility oriented toward the medically underserved and housed in a nineteenth-century building in the East Village. The design brief of the past might have called for "comfortable seating in the waiting room" or "storage unit for patient property." The brief of the design thinkers at Nurture, by contrast, is more likely to ask, "How might we create zones of privacy in public areas?" or "How might we accommodate the different spatial requirements of patients, visitors, and medical staff in a hospital recovery room?"

By shifting its focus from furniture products to the entire health care environment, Nurture represents a case study of design thinking at work. The new approach often begins with an intensive workshop called a "Deep Dive" (lighter versions are dubbed "Skinny Dips") in which product designers, interior designers, and architects team up with physicians, nurses, and patients to explore a problem, prototype possible solutions, and evaluate results. These hands-on research initiatives are typically designed to understand an issue from an industry-wide perspective, but Nurture also works on behalf of specific clients. For example, it conducted field observations on cancer care environments nationwide for the Cancer and Hematology Centers of Western Michigan and worked with the Centers' architects to build and equip a functional prototype. Before Emory University Hospital in Atlanta built a new neurological intensive care unit, it turned to Nurture for help in identifying potential design problems. The team ran simulation exercises in a mock-up of the proposed facility and also held a design charrette with the hospital's architects and clinicians, and members of patients' families to gain a better understanding of ways to include family space in the rooms of ICU patients.

Nurture's product offerings consist of reception desks, seating for waiting areas, lighting solutions for clinical laboratories, storage facilities for nurses' stations, and the like. Where it differs from the traditional design-based approach, however, is in understanding itself to be closer to the health care industry than to the contract furniture industry. Nurture begins with the premise that the physical environment contributes to the healing process as much as do prescription medicines, surgical instruments, and a skilled nursing staff. This research-based and data-driven approach has led to product innovations including enclaves in waiting rooms that allow for conversation but protect privacy through seating and modular architectural panels; nurses' stations that improve sight lines, help to manage workflows, and accommodate impromptu meetings; and patient rooms that optimize storage space, have zone lighting that meets the various needs of medical staff, visitors, and patients; and ergonomic solutions that meet the needs of radiologists and anticipate the ever-changing research methodologies of laboratory researchers.

Indeed, research scientists are not the only ones whose work is fact-based and data-driven. Together with the Mayo Clinic, Nurture has designed experiments to test its insights into clinical environments. It designed and ran a randomized controlled study to compare the effects of two different examination room designs on patient-physician interactions and—like any scrupulous research team—published the results regardless of the outcome. People who practice design thinking rely heavily upon imagination, insight, and inspiration, but at Nurture they are equally committed to the rigors of scientific procedure.

Driven by this new orientation, Steelcase designers are actively thinking not just about well-designed objects but about the workplace of the future and how to equip it. It is a sign of the times that Steelcase, whose name betrays its origins in gray metal filing cabinets, was one of the first in its industry to promote digital technology as a means of storing, retrieving, and especially sharing information. Indeed, one of the first insights to emerge from Hackett's embrace of design thinking was that many of Steelcase's client companies are themselves shifting from individual knowledge work to team-based collaboration. This trend led to important changes in the way Steelcase might support this broad structural transformation through physical space and furniture systems, but that proved to be just the beginning.

In 2000, as if to mark the coming of the digital millennium, Steelcase introduced its first fully Web-enabled product. RoomWizard, a small networked display, is designed to be mounted outside conference rooms to show who has reserved them and for how long. Operated by a simple touch screen interface or over the customer's intranet, RoomWizard allows me to reserve a meeting room in our offices in Munich or Shanghai from my laptop in Palo Alto and allows facilities managers to plan future space requirements in the most efficient way possible. Something is clearly afoot when an office furniture company begins selling networked information appliances, but facilities are supposed to facilitate, and that is what RoomWizard does. Jim Hackett continues to sell chairs, desks, and even fireproof wastebaskets, but mostly he is trying to sell solutions that will enhance the efficiency and the experience of today's workplace.

## give them the net

Back in the 1980s, IDEO did lots of work with Acer, the Taiwanese computer giant. At the end of one particularly well-received project, Professor David Liang, who had been helping us navigate the considerable cultural distance between our team and our client's team, offered the provocative counsel "They liked the fish. Next time give them the net." The deliverable, in other words, was great, but Liang saw the opportunity to share with Acer the process that had created it. Hastily we assembled a team of instructors from our design community, packed up a load of Sharpies and Post-it notes, and headed off to Taipei, where we conducted the first of what would become a major program of innovation workshops. We called it "IDEO U."

Whereas companies as far flung as McDonald's and Motorola conduct internal "universities" to train their own employees, we turned outward and set out to train companies in our methods of human-centered, design-based innovation: user observations, brainstorming, prototyping, storytelling, and scenario building. Over time, however, and after countless workshops conducted throughout the world, we learned that planting a cell of design-trained, innovation-minded conspirators inside a large organization is not the most effective way to proceed. Innovation needs to be coded into the DNA of a company if it is to have large-scale, long-term impact.

As the concept evolved, we began to run more structured workshops focused around the specific objectives of companies including Nestlé, P&G, and Kraft Foods. Still, in the absence of broader organizational changes the impact of a stand-alone workshop will be limited. All the innovation workshops in the world would not have transformed P&G if A. G. Lafley had not designated a chief innovation officer, increased the number of design managers by more than 500 percent, built the P&G Innovation Gym, created a new approach to partnering with the outside world ("Connect and Develop"), and elevated innovation and design to core strategies of the company.

Companies such as P&G, Hewlett-Packard, and Steelcase that make products and manage brands have a head start when it comes to transforming their internal cultures because they already have designers, and even some design thinkers, on their payrolls. Though it may be difficult to convince management of the merits of a more strategic role for design, once they are convinced there is often a base of talent already in place. In service organizations, or even manufacturing companies where design has traditionally been outsourced, that base may not exist and the challenge is greater.

The giant health care provider Kaiser Permanente is a case in point. In 2003, Kaiser set out to improve the overall quality of the health care experience from the point of view of both patients and medical practitioners. IDEO proposed that rather than hire a slew of internal designers, the existing staff should learn the principles of design thinking and apply them themselves. Over the course of several months we conducted a series of workshops with nurses, doctors, and administrators that led to a portfolio of innovations. One of them—a project to reengineer nursing staff shift changes—involved a strategist with a nursing background, a specialist in organizational development, a technology expert, a process designer, and a union representative, facilitated by designers from IDEO.

Working with frontline caregivers at each of four Kaiser hospitals, the core team identified the problems that occur when shifts change. Departing nurses routinely spent forty-five minutes briefing the arriving shift about the status of their patients. The procedures were unsystematic and differed from hospital to hospital—from recorded dictation to face-to-face meetings—and methods used for compiling information varied from the frantic use of Post-it notes to information scrawled on hospital scrubs. Knowledge that patients cared about was often lost: how they had progressed during the previous shift, which family members were with them, which tests and therapies had been completed. The team learned that many patients felt that the shift change created a hole in their care. What followed from these observations were the now-familiar elements of a robust design process—brainstorming, prototyping, role playing, videotaping—carried out not by professional designers but by Kaiser's own staff.

The result was a change in approach, with nurses exchanging information in front of the patient instead of back at the nurses' station. The first prototype, built in only a week, included new procedures and simple software that enabled nurses to call up previous shift-change notes and add new ones throughout their shifts. More important, patients were now part of the process and could bring up additional details that were important to them. Kaiser measured the impact of this change and found that the mean time between a nurse's arriving on shift and first interacting with a patient was more than halved. The innovation also had an impact on how nurses felt about their job. In a survey, one commented, "I'm an hour ahead, and I've only been here forty-five minutes." Another was excited that this was the "first time I've ever made it out of here at the end of my shift."

The new nurse shift change had an impact on patients and nurses but on its own was a long way from achieving the desired goal of a systematic improvement in the overall quality of health care at Kaiser. To achieve that, the core team of nurses, development experts, and technologists went from carrying out their own projects to acting as consultants to the rest of the organization. Through the establishment of the Kaiser Permanente Innovation Consultancy the team pursues the mission of enhancing the patient experience, envisioning Kaiser's "hospital of the future," and introducing innovation and design thinking across the Kaiser system.

It takes a systematic approach to achieve organizationwide change. Initiating nurses and administrators (or executives and clerks, or branch managers and bank tellers . . . ) into the mysteries of design thinking can unleash passion and energy and creativity. At Kaiser it resulted in literally dozens of innovative ideas that were ready to be rolled out across the entire hospital system. It can also elicit new levels of engagement from people who may have spent so much time fighting the system that they could barely imagine having a role in redesigning it. But without a sustained commitment and an integrated approach, the initial effort might have been overwhelmed by the day-to-day exigencies of running a complex health care system.

The transformation of a business-as-usual culture into one focused on innovation and driven by design involves activities, decisions, and attitudes. Workshops help expose people to design thinking as a new approach. Pilot projects help market the benefits of design thinking within the organization. Leadership focuses the program of change and gives people permission to learn and experiment. Assembling interdisciplinary teams ensures that the effort is broadly based. Dedicated spaces such as the P&G Innovation Gym provide a resource for longer-term thinking and ensure that the effort will be sustained. Measurement of impacts, both quantitative and qualitative, helps make the business case and ensures that resources are appropriately allocated. It may make sense to establish incentives for business units to collaborate in new ways so that younger talent sees innovation as a path to success rather than as a career risk.

Were all these elements to work together in harmony, the gears of innovation would turn smoothly. It is not so easy in the face of the real-world challenges confronted every day. Individual business units are focused on immediate concerns, and it can be hard to persuade them to participate in systemwide innovation initiatives. We all know how difficult it can be to keep faith in a volatile business environment in which short-term obstacles seem more demanding than long-term objectives. Too many executives panic at the first sign of bad news. Innovation is not something to be turned on and off like a faucet. Breakthrough ideas take longer to germinate than it takes for all but the longest and deepest recessions take to pass. Companies that suspend innovation efforts, lay off staff, and kill projects as they enter a downturn will only weaken their innovation pipeline. They may need to refocus their efforts and run their projects with fewer resources, but cutting them off altogether leaves them at risk of being blindsided when markets recover.

An idea incubated in a downturn may have massive impact when times improve. As Andrew Razeghi has recently shown, *Fortune* magazine was launched just four months after the stock market crash of October 1929 at the high price of $1 per issue and to a small market of only 30,000 subscribers; by 1937, circulation was 460,000, with net profits of $500,000.

Other instances followed, including instant coffee, budget airlines, and the iPod. Razeghi argues that new needs are easier to spot in a downturn than in a boom, where there is a surfeit of great ideas chasing needs that have already been met. This conclusion indicates that design thinking may be one of the most profitable practices a corporation can adopt during a recession.

In the 1950s, W. Edwards Deming began to plant the study of quality on rigorous foundations. Design thinking is unlikely to become an exact science, but as with the quality movement there is an opportunity to transform it from a black art into a systematically applied management approach. The trick is to do this without sucking the life out of the creative process—to balance management's legitimate requirement for stability, efficiency, and predictability with the design thinker's need for spontaneity, serendipity, and experimentation. The objective, as the University of Toronto's Roger Martin reminds us, should be integration: holding these conflicting demands in tension while we create innovations, and indeed companies, that are more powerful than either of them.

# the new social contract,
## or *we're all in this together*

An organization that commits itself to the human-centered tenets of design thinking is practicing enlightened self-interest. If it does a better job of understanding its customers, it will do a better job of satisfying their needs. That is simply the most reliable source of long-term profitability and sustainable growth. In the world of business, every idea—however noble—must survive the test of the bottom line.

But this is not a one-sided proposition. Businesses are taking a more human-centered approach because people's expectations are evolving. Whether we find ourselves in the role of customer or client, patient or passenger, we are no longer content to be passive consumers at the far end of the industrial economy. For some this leads to a quest for more meaningful pursuits than "getting and spending." For others it may take the form of holding companies accountable for the impact of their products upon our bodies, our culture, and our environment. The net effect, however, is a far-reaching shift in the dynamic between sellers of goods and providers of services, and those who purchase them.

As consumers we are making new and different sorts of demands; we relate differently to brands; we expect to participate in determining what will be offered to us; and we expect our relationship with manufacturers and sellers to continue beyond the point of purchase. To meet these heightened expectations, companies have to yield some of their sovereign authority over the market and enter into a two-way conversation with their customers. This shift is happening at three levels, and they will shape the argument of this chapter. First, there is a seemingly inexorable blurring of the line between "products" and "services," as consumers shift from the expectation of functional performance to a more broadly satisfying experience. Second, design thinking is being applied at new scales in the move from discrete products and services to complex systems. Third, there is a dawning recognition among manufacturers, consumers, and everyone in between that we are entering an era of limits; the cycle of mass production and mindless consumption that defined the industrial age is no longer sustainable.

These trends converge around a single, inescapable point: design thinking needs to be turned toward the formulation of a new participatory social contract. It is no longer possible to think in adversarial terms of a "buyer's market" or a "seller's market." We're all in this together.

## the shift to services

In some sense, every product is already a service. However inert it may seem, a product implies a prior association with the brand that stands behind it and carries the expectation of the maintenance, repair, or upgrade that will follow once we have purchased it. By the same token, few services do not include something tangible, whether it be the airplane seat that carries us across a continent or the BlackBerry that connects us to a vast network of telecommunications services. The line between product and service has become blurred. Some companies—Virgin Atlantic Airways, the European mobile operator Orange, Four Seasons Hotels and Resorts—have been quicker to recognize this than their competitors and have been rewarded by a loyal customer following.

It is surprising, then, that service businesses have been so much slower to innovate than companies that produce office furniture, consumer electronics, or sportswear. Few of them have built strong research and development cultures. Their business operations are rarely informed by the strategies that have proven so successful elsewhere.

The core of the problem is that the manufacturing sector deals with machines and the service sector deals with people. This is a rather gross oversimplification, of course, but it rests on a principle that is quite complex. Industrialization was driven by sweeping innovations in technology. One need only dip into the novels of Charles Dickens, Émile Zola, or D. H. Lawrence to observe how people were dragged along in its wake. Companies competed with one another on the basis of their technological prowess and adopted practices designed to increase their capacity for technological innovation. As small start-ups grew into industrial empires such as General Electric, Siemens, and Krups, they established research labs, design studios, university affiliations, and other means of systematizing innovation. Historians such as David Noble and Thomas Parke Hughes have tracked how new forms of intellectual property—patents, copyrights, and licensing arrangements of every imaginable sort—were tied to the growth of these new megacompanies. Even governments took on the role of protectors of intellectual property as a matter of national competitiveness: Britain in the 1850s, Germany in the 1910s, Japan in the 1950s, and China today.

Investing in a future stream of technical innovation became part of the management of the large industrial company. Thomas Edison led the way with the opening of the first modern industrial research lab—the so-called invention factory—in 1876, and research and development has been part of manufacturing companies ever since. Though they may not be quite as ambitious as "the Wizard of Menlo Park"—Edison famously promised a minor invention every ten days or so and a "big trick" every six months—most manufacturing companies assume that the way to ensure a stream of products tomorrow is to invest in technological research today.

Investment in innovation continues to grow and evolve. It now includes a variety of models. Apple Inc. does not maintain a large research facility, but it does invest hundreds of millions of dollars every year in the design and engineering of new products. Procter & Gamble maintains a large commitment to R&D but also invests heavily in consumer-centered innovation and design. Toyota, the world's biggest automaker, is famous for investing in process innovation to improve the quality of its manufacturing. Product companies are so dependent on their stream of new ideas that the stock market often values them on their commitment to innovation. Why is this not the case with the service sector?

Among service companies one rarely finds a culture built around investing in future innovations. Where it does exist, it tends to be concentrated on the infrastructure that makes a service possible rather than the service itself. Telecommunications companies invested in copper wire–based networks and then in mobile technology, but they paid little attention to the customer experience. AT&T built one of the most famous research laboratories of them all, but even during its heyday Bell Labs behaved more like a manufacturer of telephones than a provider of telecommunications services.

In the Main Street world of retailing, food services, banking, insurance, and even health care, there was little thought given to systematic innovation before the advent of home computing and more specifically the Internet. Citibank gained its reputation as one of the most innovative financial institutions in 1977 when it installed networked ATMs in its branches around New York. This radical service innovation allowed customers to do their banking on their own terms. For the first time since the invention of the slot machine, a piece of technology got between us and our money, and many people had a difficult time with that. Eleanor Wetzel, whose husband invented it, claims never to have used one.

Prior to the computer and the Internet, almost every service relied on direct interaction between the service provider and the service recipient. In this people-to-people world, a company's competitiveness rested on how well service personnel could look after their customers. This translated into a simple formula: the more premium a service, the more people were generally involved in delivering it. A luxury hotel had more bellboys, concierge staff, cleaners, and cooks per customer. A premium private bank gave its wealthy customers one-on-one service rather than forcing them to line up for a teller like the rest of us. As long as it was people who determined the quality of the service customers received, there was little incentive to think about the sort of breakthrough service innovations that could redefine a market.

Of course, there are exceptions. Isadore Sharp created Four Seasons on the premise that large-scale hotels and great service were not incompatible. Howard Schultz built Starbucks into a global brand on the insight that ambience is as important to coffee drinkers as caffeine. Whether he is selling records, bridal wear, or airplane tickets, Sir Richard Branson recognizes the centrality of the service experience.

By the end of the 1990s, many companies had finally acknowledged that technology was destined to replace, or at least significantly augment the role of people in defining the consumer experience. In just a few years, companies such as Amazon, Zappos, and Netflix went from untested start-ups to major brands. eBay went one step further, creating a clever infrastructure that enabled customers to do all of the work and charging them for the privilege of doing so. Other sectors recognized that these new networks offered huge potential. Dell found that it didn't need to rely on archaic electronics stores to distribute its computers. Instead it went direct to the customer. Wal-Mart used computer networks to manage a gigantic group of suppliers with a level of efficiency never before seen and at the lowest possible price. Suddenly, it seemed, service companies were competing based on their leverage of technology and not just of people. Competitiveness became dependent on innovation.

At the same time, not all service-sector companies have gone on to discover the hard-won lesson learned by their manufacturing counterparts: technology alone does not necessarily result in a better customer experience. Coming from the British Midlands, I sometimes think of the interminable loops of telephone answering systems or the confounding Web sites of so many e-tailers as the modern-day equivalent of the "dark satanic mills" that haunted the imagination of William Blake during the first throes of the industrial revolution. They subordinate humans to the inscrutable logic of the machine; they degrade and frustrate us; they compromise the quality of life and the efficiency of work. Service companies that use innovative technology but do not innovate to improve the quality of people's experience are destined to relearn the bitter lesson of the companies of the industrial age: that past innovation is no guarantee of future performance.

Netflix is one service company that understands this. During its first few years, once it had launched its breakthrough innovation of renting DVDs via the Internet and having them delivered by the postal service, Netflix focused on building its core proposition and securing a customer base large enough to sustain it. Early experiments were incremental and focused on improving the usability of its Web site and tinkering with different subscription levels. Next the company began identifying networks of trends and providing subscribers with a repository of film data and rankings. More recently it has begun experimenting with what is probably the inevitable shift to using the Internet not just as a sales counter but as an online movie delivery system. This first required downloading movies and watching them on a home computer, but technology is advancing. The California-based company Roku builds a set-top box that allows people to download movies and watch them on a standard television. The South Korean giant LG Electronics has Netflix-downloading capability built into its standard Blu-ray players. With every advance, Netflix has focused on the design of the experience and not just the technology. There is still a long way to go before thousands of letter carriers no longer drop millions of red envelopes into mailboxes, but Netflix has begun to guide its customers on a gradual journey without frustrating them, alienating them, or losing them along the way.

Just as products become more like services, services are becoming more like experiences. Underlying this profound and inevitable evolution is an understanding of the importance of investing in systematic, design-based innovation that engages people—both employees and customers—at the deepest level. Eventually it will be as natural to see innovation labs in service-sector companies as it is to see research and development facilities in manufacturing companies.

## systems at scale and why we should act more like honeybees

Every design challenge at IDEO begins with a "How Might We?" Navigating between the overly general and the too specific, we ask ourselves, "HMW simplify the interface on an emergency heart defibrillator? HMW encourage healthy snacking among preteens? HMW promote the revival of a historic jazz district in Kansas City?" "How might we improve the human condition?" is too big a problem to get our arms around. "How might we adjust the tension in a disk-drive eject mechanism?" is probably too small.

Here is a good one: how might we improve the airport-security experience? Airport security is one of the challenges that every design thinker must have thought about a hundred times since September 11, 2001—I certainly do every time I struggle to take my shoes off and put them onto the conveyor belt without holding up traffic, share the indignity of my Indian traveling companion as he pretends to ignore furtive glances in his direction, or watch somebody's forgetful grandmother surrender her shampoo bottle to an apologetic officer. It is hard for me as a designer *not* to think about how we might better meet our legitimate need for security in the post-9/11 world. As both a citizen and a designer, I was thrilled when the U.S. Transportation Security Administration (TSA) came and asked us that very question.

Our work with the TSA proved to be among the most challenging assignments in IDEO's thirty-year history. It illustrates how design thinking has to move into the hands of all participants if we are to improve the performance of our large-scale systems.

Reconfiguring the space and flow of the checkpoint will certainly make for an easier traveling experience by giving passengers more time to organize themselves and providing a better informational context for what is going on. The space is just the physical dimension of a larger systemic problem, however. The key idea was to move upstream and rethink the manner in which passenger and Transportation Security Officer (TSO) participate in a common experience.

TSA was attempting to redirect its focus from the detection of objects to the detection of hostile intent: a pair of sharp manicure scissors in a lady's purse poses little threat, whereas an empty soft drink can—as a TSA official demonstrated, to the consternation of one of our designers—can be made into a lethal weapon. A set of top-down regulations issued from Washington was not enough to bring this about, however. To implement the new *security* strategy, a comprehensive new *design* strategy seemed essential.

The guiding principle for any systemwide project on this scale is to ensure that the objectives of different participants are aligned. In the case of airport security, this insight meant recognizing that security personnel and the traveling public are not adversaries but partners, whose respective goals—to spot likely terrorists and to get to their departure gates quickly and with minimum stress—are complementary. Taking the stress out of the normal passenger experience makes it easier to spot abnormal behaviors of those who might do us harm (if everyone in the queue is nervous and agitated, the malefactor with a bomb in his shoe will blend right in). This became the framework within which we pressed forward with concrete proposals for how we might streamline processes and modify environments.

In the observation phase of our research we saw how passengers, confronted with opaque procedural rules, become anxious, aggressive, and uncooperative. TSOs, for their part, responded by retreating into scripted roles that made them appear intimidating, aloof, and unsympathetic. A vicious circle of inefficiency and unpleasantness is the result, and to the extent that an adversarial climate creates unnecessary distractions, it actually impedes the common goal of safe travel. Thus the designer's question—"How might we reconfigure the security checkpoint?"—evolved into the *design thinker's* question "How might we instill a feeling of empathy in participants on *both* sides of the X-ray machine?" Our physical design solutions became tactics in the service of a broader, human-centered strategy.

This led us in two parallel directions. First, we created a program of environmental and informational design elements designed to smooth the transition from lobby to final checkpoint and brought to life in a working prototype in Baltimore Washington International Airport. The physical layout and information displays were designed to explain as much as possible about what to expect. If passengers understand what is being asked of them and why, they are more likely to be tolerant of procedures that might otherwise seem pointless and arbitrary. At the same time, however, we helped create for TSA officers a training program designed to give them authority to engage the system in a new way. It encourages a broadening out from rote-based procedures to a more flexible yet rigorous reliance on critical thinking. The new training includes an emphasis on understanding behavior, people, and security measures, while instilling confidence among colleagues and passengers.

Much has been written about complex nonhierarchical systems in which the behavior of the system is the result not of centralized command and control but of a set of individual behaviors that, when repeated thousands of times, achieve predictable results. Anthills and beehives are good examples, but when it comes to colonies of humans, we have to reckon with the additional factors of individual intelligence and free will (often to the despair of designers, police officers, and high school teachers). The implication is that we must think differently. Instead of an inflexible, hierarchical process that is designed once and executed many times, we must imagine how we might create highly flexible, constantly evolving systems in which each exchange between participants is an opportunity for empathy, insight, innovation, and implementation. Every interaction is a small opportunity to make that exchange more valuable to and meaningful for all participants.

Colonies of bees, ants, and humans must adapt and evolve if they are to be successful, and one way to achieve this is to empower individuals with some degree of control over the end result. In the case of TSA, this proved to be a powerful argument for the design thinker's gambit of handing off the tools of design to the people who will ultimately be responsible for implementing them.

## working both sides of the counter

One does not have to grapple with the extraordinary challenges of asymmetrical warfare, nonstate actors, and terrorism to see value in the empathic approach of the design thinker. In 2004 Julie Gilbert, the vice president of customer centricity at Best Buy, created the Women's Leadership Forum, known as WOLF. Each "WOLF Pack" consists of twenty-five women and two men who come together from all parts of the organization to focus on challenges arising in a retail industry built by men and for men but in which 45 percent of all purchases are made by women. As a result of their efforts—which have involved more than 20,000 customers and employees—there has been an increase in female job applicants of 37% and a nearly 6% decrease in female employee turnover. Women—again, on both sides of the counter—have become active coparticipants in transforming Best Buy as a place to shop and to work. Initiatives include widening aisles so that baby strollers can fit down them, whittling the stacks of equipment down to make the environment less intimidating, and displaying wide-screen TVs and surround-sound systems in living room mock-ups so that shoppers can see what the products will look like in their home. Instead of intimidating customers with performance features, staff is now trained to talk to them about their lifestyles and what they want the technology to do for them.

Toyota's total immersion training program demonstrates the same commitment to softening the distinctions—between management and employees, between customer and staff. Toyota is, in effect, training its leaders to listen and its employees to speak up, to the advantage of both. The management consultant Steven J. Spear has observed how a new Toyota plant manager experiences his first few weeks on the job by working directly on the manufacturing line. The American manager, who could not speak Japanese, spent a week working alongside a Japanese production worker with no English; using a common language of observation, prototyping, and role playing, they identified solutions to more than thirty-five production problems, ranging from reducing the distance a worker had to walk to check a part by 50 percent to improving the ergonomics of a tool change, and fixed them on the spot. By redefining the role of leaders and employees, Toyota promotes a level of collaboration unimaginable in most Western-run industrial companies. Spear identifies four principles fundamental to Toyota's success with total immersion training: "There's no substitute for direct observation"; "Proposed changes should always be structured as experiments"; "Workers and managers should experiment as frequently as possible"; "Managers should coach, not fix." Observation? Prototyping? Experiment? Throw in a brainstorming session or two, and you have a pretty accurate description of a culture in which design thinking has moved out of the studio and into the boardroom and the factory floor.

Sometimes, as with Toyota, the principles of design thinking are formulated explicitly. In other instances it takes the form of a more generalized commitment to the alignment of system and participants. In January 2000, Jimmy Wales and Larry Sanger began to create a free, online encyclopedia with content supplied by volunteers. Their initial approach was quite conventional: accredited experts would submit articles for peer review. After nine months this careful process had generated exactly twelve articles.

By chance the team had learned about wiki software, a type of collaborative, open-source Web site launched by the programmer Ward Cunningham about five years earlier that allows anyone to modify its content without consulting some centralized authority. Wales had the idea to use this new tool to speed up the process of getting articles for the encyclopedia. Wikipedia was launched in January 2001, inviting users to submit articles directly. Within a month they had one thousand articles. By September, ten thousand. Wikipedia is today by far the largest publication on the Net, providing references for almost every high school paper and business book in existence (including this one). By positioning Wikipedia as a nonprofit foundation rather than a business, Jimmy Wales held to his core principle that unpaid contributors are crucial to the enterprise. Its entries are created by people who care about the content, rather than by paid professionals, which gives Wikipedia its credibility, controls its quality, and ensures its relevance. Wikipedia is a testament to the power of participation in a system whose participants are aligned in their objectives.

It is instructive to compare the successes of Wikipedia, Toyota, and Best Buy with some of the broken systems we encounter in our everyday lives. The ordeal of renewing a driving license, negotiating with a health insurance provider, or voting in an election suggests that too many of our large-scale systems fail to deliver a respectful, efficient, participatory experience. We might resign ourselves to the ponderous workings of government bureaucracies, but we should not forgive the companies we patronize for their decided lack of imagination.

Every media company that resists the digitization of content, every mobile service provider that forces us to buy services from a single source, every bank that exacts outrageous fees opens up opportunities for more agile and imaginative competitors. The open-source platform Android, now owned by Google, is a good example of a disruptive innovation that is poised to dislodge more established mobile phone providers. Thousands of developers are already working on Android applications, far outstripping the capabilities of Google's in-house development teams, and the first G-phones operating the Android operating system are appearing on the market. Demand is outstripping supply. In banking, another industry whose titans are falling from power, online social lending institutions such as Zopa, are taking a new approach. Zopa's direct, peer-to-peer model sidesteps the banks and helps potential borrowers and lenders find a "zone of possible agreement" between them. Since its founding in 2005, Zopa has spread from its base in Britain to the United States, Italy, and Japan and has achieved remarkably low default rates.

The idea of participation is attractive but not sufficient. No one wants to use a poorly designed mobile application or deposit a paycheck in an insecure bank, no matter how "participatory" it may feel. These new kinds of systems must also deliver high-quality performance that is at least as good as that of companies that rely on a top-down approach. Android applications will have to be as engaging and intuitive as those from Apple and Nokia, or they will remain the preserve of open-source techno-geeks, and Zopa's customers must be assured that their money is safe. This confidence does not come from a network administrator. If open, flexible, large-scale systems are to realize their enormous promise, their developers must have the courage to open them up to the people who will use them. *Design* is about delivering a satisfying experience. *Design thinking* is about creating a multipolar experience in which everyone has the opportunity to participate in the conversation.

## the future of companies, economies, and Planet Earth

What all of these themes and examples have in common is direct engagement with people—whether they happen to be customers, clients, members of an audience, or solitary viewers of a Web site. The widespread shift, even among traditional manufacturing companies, from a "product" orientation to a "service" orientation is key to scaling up the tools of the design thinker to grapple with complex systems on the order of airport security. It is the very essence of open-source, social networking and Web 2.0.

Having looked at systems designed to move travelers through airports, products through markets, and electrons through the encyclopedic virtual world of the Internet, we can now turn to the biggest system of them all: the fragile, beautiful, delicately balanced life-support system that Buckminster Fuller called "Spaceship Earth." If a task ever required the combination of analytic and synthetic practices, divergent and convergent thought, the designer's mastery of technology and insight into human behavior, preserving the health of our planet would be it. Holding the economic sustainability of society and the biological sustainability of the planet in balance requires the most "opposable" of minds.

As a designer, I am proud that we have helped create better products that meet people's needs and help humanize the technology they rely on. We have better buildings that allow us to live and work more comfortably. We have innovative media that inform and entertain us and allow us to communicate with one another in undreamed-of ways. But we also have a Pandora's box of unanticipated problems that may have already contributed to long-term damage to our culture, our economy, and our environment.

Some years ago a talented team at IDEO worked with Oral-B to design a better children's toothbrush. The team began with an intensive research phase, going into the field to watch kids of all ages clean their teeth—or at least try to. One reason why children struggle to keep their teeth healthy is that brushing teeth is not an activity that most kids would choose to do. It hurts. It's not fun. It tastes funny. Another is that young children do not have the manual dexterity to hold a toothbrush. Most children's toothbrushes were scaled-down versions of those designed for adults (like the Dutch Masters of the seventeenth century, industrial designers of the twentieth century simply treated children as miniature adults). The solution led to the first toothbrushes with the squishy "comolded" rubber handles that are now the norm for all toothbrushes, for both children and adults. The team also gave the Oral-B brushes bright colors, bold textures, and forms evoking turtles and dinosaurs. The new toothbrushes were a huge hit.

Oral-B had a successful product, and lots of kids had healthier teeth. But this is just the "front end" of the story. Just six months after its launch, the lead designer in this group was walking along an isolated beach in Baja California and noticed a colorful blue object lying just out of reach of the surf. It was not a turtle. One of our ergonomically designed, dentist-approved, commercially successful Oral-B toothbrushes had washed up on shore. With the exception of some tiny barnacles that indicated that it had been in the water for some time, the toothbrush looked more or less the same as it had on the day someone had thrown it away. The circle closed. One of our signature products had found its final resting place on a pristine beach in Mexico.

Designers can't prevent people from doing what they want to with products they own, but that does not excuse them from ignoring the larger system. Often, in our enthusiasm for solving the problem in front of us, we fail to see the problems that we create. Designers, and people who aspire to think like designers, are in a position to make important decisions about what resources society uses and where they end up.

There are at least three significant areas where design thinking can promote what the Canadian designer Bruce Mau calls the "massive change" that is called for today. The first has to do with informing ourselves about what is at stake and making visible the true costs of the choices we make. The second involves a fundamental reassessment of the systems and processes we use to create new things. The third task to which design thinking must respond is to find ways to encourage individuals to move toward more sustainable behaviors.

## informing ourselves

Environmentalism entered the cultural mainstream with the publication of Rachel Carson's *Silent Spring* in 1962, but it would take another forty years—after two oil crises and a broad scientific consensus—for a general awareness of the crisis to sink in. A major stimulus was the release of Al Gore's documentary, *An Inconvenient Truth*, in 2006, an event that suggests the power of imagery to motivate fundamental change. Together with the fact-based investigations of journalists, the data-driven analyses of scientists, and the politically inspired activism of communities, the work of visual artists can play a vital role in moving us back from the precipice.

Chris Jordan is an American artist who uses the power of scale to connect us to many different social issues. His series *Picturing Excess* includes images such as a five-by-ten-foot representation of the number of plastic water bottles—about 2 million—consumed in the United States every five minutes. Another composition depicts 426,000 cell phones—the number retired by Americans every day. The visual impact of his work exposes our profligate use of the earth's finite resources in a way that words cannot.

Another artist, the Canadian Edward Burtynsky, has traveled the planet recording the beauty and the horror of human impact. Burtynsky's large-format photographs draw the viewer into the lives of Chinese villagers breaking apart used computer monitors with hammers or laboring in the cavernous factories of Shenzhen. The eerie beauty of orange tailings snaking across the landscape from the nickel mines of Ontario conveys the scale of our activities in a way that is visceral and emotional.

The vast photographic landscapes of Edward Burtynsky and the intricate visualizations of data conceived by Chris Jordan overwhelm us with scale, but design thinkers have also shown that it is possible to approach the challenge of sustainability at a more immediately accessible level. As director of the global foresight and innovation initiative at the engineering firm Arup, Dr. Chris Luebkeman created decks of cards he calls Drivers of Change. Each mutually reinforcing set covers a major category of environmental change—climate, energy, urbanization, waste, water, and demographics—with each card illustrating a single driver for change from a different perspective: society, technology, economics, environment, and politics. By means of imagery, graphs, and a few well-chosen facts, each card gives a clear picture of a single issue without overloading the viewer's capacity to absorb and understand. One asks, "How important are trees?" and goes on to explain the issue of carbon emissions from deforestation. Another asks, "Can we afford a low carbon future?" and explains the impact of developing economies on carbon output. Arup uses Drivers of Change as a tool for discussion groups, as personal prompts, for workshop events, or simply as an inspirational "thought for the week." By thinking like a designer and using insights as a source of inspiration,

Luebkeman has created a valuable tool that may inspire other design thinkers in their search for solutions.

## doing more with less

Pangea Organics—"pangea" means "whole earth"—is a small company based in Boulder, Colorado, that makes natural body care products. After four years in operation Pangea soaps, lotions, and shampoos could be found in natural food stores within a limited range, and its founder, Joshua Onysko, began to think about how to grow the company without compromising the core environmental values on which it was based. A competent designer might have proposed a nationwide advertising campaign complete with eye-catching packaging and a more mainstream message. A team of design thinkers, however, saw the brief more broadly: it was not just about selling soap but about selling the idea of sustainability, wellness, and responsibility.

Taking into account Pangea's need for a viable business strategy and its customers' desire for products that made them feel like responsible custodians of the earth, the team turned to the question of what was feasible within the constraints of low cost and minimum environmental impact. The result was a comprehensive rebranding that leads customers on a journey not from factory to landfill but rather, to borrow the words of the architect and designer William McDonough, from "cradle to cradle." Just as the "packaging" of a banana becomes a nutrient for the next generation of trees, the new compostable carton for Pangea's soaps is embedded with wildflower seeds: soak it in water, toss it into your backyard, come back a few days later to find a garden.

The author Janine Benyus, who has popularized the concept of biomimicry, has observed that the industrial age was founded on the triadic principle of "heat, beat, and treat." This muscular approach has to be replaced by alternatives that are far less intrusive and wasteful and whose inspiration is more biological than mechanical. The brief being handed to design thinkers today is to find new ways of balancing desirability, feasibility, and viability, but in a way that closes the loop.

What Pangea Organics is attempting to do on a small scale, Amory Lovins wants to do for the whole of the automobile industry. Lovins does not start by asking how we might design a more appealing or even economical car. He and his colleagues at the Rocky Mountain Institute (RMI) have framed the question with different parameters, more akin to the tenets of design thinking than of design: "How do we get to a three- to five-fold increase in fuel economy, equal or better performance, safety, amenity, and affordability compared to today's vehicles?" From this human-centered, systemswide brief they arrived at the Hypercar, a vehicle that makes use of advanced composites, low-drag design, hybrid electric drive, and efficient accessories. RMI set up the Hypercar Center in 1994 to prototype ideas, and the institute now has a for-profit company, Fiberforge, that is developing advanced composites to support this effort. By thinking upstream, beyond the artifact, RMI formulated a different design problem from the one that most automotive companies concern themselves with today. In the past there was a streak of utopianism in RMI's quixotic campaign, but the precarious state of the automotive industry may help to pull such efforts in from the margins.

If we take time to examine the whole cycle of creation and use of a product—from the extraction of raw materials used in manufacturing to disposal at the end of its useful life—we may be able to find new opportunities for innovation that reduce environmental impact while enhancing rather than diminishing the quality of life we have come to expect. By thinking in terms of the whole system, companies can capture bigger opportunities. But we can't stop there. Design thinkers must also consider the demand side of the equation.

## altering our behaviors

The SUV may be the defining artifact of our time. More than any other product, it embodies the nature of corporations to respond to what people want, usually with more of the same—in this case *much* more—no matter what the cost. The popularity of these dangerous, expensive, inefficient, and ecologically disastrous vehicles demonstrates that change needs to happen simultaneously at the level of demand and supply. We need to find ways to encourage people to see energy conservation as more of an investment than a sacrifice, as so many have when they resolved to give up cigarettes, lose weight, or save for retirement.

The U.S. Department of Energy understood this when officials in its Office of Energy Efficiency and Renewable Energy (EERE) used design thinking to broaden their efforts. DoE had traditionally begun with the assumption that people already care about energy efficiency and directed its resources toward R&D programs whose fruits—new energy-efficient technologies—would satisfy this demand. In a program code-named Shift Focus, IDEO proposed a new, human-centered approach that began by questioning this assumption.

After an intensive period of field research, in which the IDEO team sampled consumer opinion in Mobile, Dallas, Phoenix, Boston, Juneau, and Detroit, it came to an arresting conclusion: people do not care about energy efficiency. This does not mean that the public is ignorant, profligate, or irresponsible but that "energy efficiency" is an abstraction that is at best a means of achieving goals that people really do care about: comfort, style, community. This finding led the design team to recommend that DoE shift from finding engineering solutions to people's presumed needs to finding ways to engage them at the level of their actual values and at meaningful points in their lives. The design proposals that followed built upon these foundations: stylish but thermally efficient window coverings, retail displays of energy-efficient lighting, informational and educational tools to capitalize upon people's heightened receptivity at moments of change such as buying a new house or upgrading their utilities.

We are in the midst of an epochal shift in the balance of power as economies evolve from a focus on manufactured products to one that favors services and experiences. Companies are ceding control and coming to see their customers not as "end users" but rather as participants in a two-way process. What is emerging is nothing less that a new social contract.

Every contract, however, has two parties. If people do not wish companies to treat them like passive consumers, they must step up to the controls and assume their fair share of responsibility. This means that we cannot sit back and wait for new choices to emerge from the inner sanctum of corporate marketing departments, R&D labs, and design studios. The implications are clear: the public, too, must commit to the principles of design thinking, just like the nurses at Kaiser, the production workers at Toyota, the WOLF Packs at Best Buy, and the public servants at the Transportation Security Administration and the Department of Energy.

As the circle of design thinkers grows, we will see solutions evolving that will improve the character of the products and services we buy. Even on a large scale and even at the level of the most challenging problems we face in our society today, design thinking can provide guidance. Left to its own, the vicious circle of design-manufacture-marketing-consumption will exhaust itself and Spaceship Earth will run out of fuel. With the active participation of people at every level, we may just be able to extend this journey for a while longer.

# design activism,
## or *inspiring solutions with global potential*

A half century ago Raymond Loewy boasted of his role in boosting the sales of Lucky Strike cigarettes by fiddling with the graphics on the box. Few designers today would even touch this type of project. The rise of design thinking corresponds to a culture change, and what excites the best thinkers today is the challenge of applying their skills to problems that matter. Improving the lives of people in extreme need is near the top of that list.

This is not merely a matter of collective altruism. The greatest design thinkers have always been drawn to the greatest challenges, whether delivering fresh water to Imperial Rome, vaulting the dome of the Florence Cathedral, running a rail line through the British Midlands, or designing the first laptop computer. They have searched out the problems that allowed them to work at the edge because this was where they were most likely to achieve something that has not been done before. For the last generation of designers, those problems were driven by new technologies. For the next generation, the most pressing—and the most exciting—challenges may lie in the highlands of southeast Asia, the malarial wetlands of East Africa, the favelas and rain forests of Brazil, and the melting glaciers of Greenland.

I do not mean to suggest that designers have never before

taken on problems at the scale of sustainability and global poverty. Victor Papanek's *Design for the Real World* was required reading when I entered art school three decades ago, and I still recall our late-night discussions about design being for "people, not profit." Out of this righteous indignation came any number of tin-can radios and emergency shelters, but apart from a dawning consciousness of our social responsibilities, there is little evidence of its having had a lasting impact. The reason is that as designers we focused our skills on the object in question and ignored the rest of the system: Who will use it, how, and under what circumstances? How will it be manufactured, distributed, and maintained? Will it support cultural traditions or disrupt them?

A better model is that developed by Martin Fisher, a Stanford PhD who was denied a Fulbright scholarship to work in Peru because he didn't speak Spanish. Fisher reluctantly agreed to a ten-month assignment in Kenya, where he ended up staying for seventeen years. In Nairobi he observed that people in poor countries who have been thrust into the global economy do not need money so much as the means to earn money. Together with his development partner Nick Moon, Fisher founded KickStart, a provider of low-cost "microtechnologies" including a treadle-operated deepwater pump—significantly called the "Super MoneyMaker"—that have helped more than 80,000 local farmers launch small businesses in East Africa. Fisher understood that the ingenious pumps, brick presses, and palm-oil extractors were not enough. His customers needed a local infrastructure including marketing, distribution, and maintenance. Educated in the high-technology world of Silicon Valley and schooled in the slums of Nairobi, Fisher shows how design thinking extends the perimeter around a problem.

## the most extreme users of them all

When Hewlett-Packard asked IDEO to study microfinance in East Africa, our human factors experts did not know what they were getting into. We did not have much experience with Africa, and it would be generous to say that we are experts in microfinance. So of course we accepted the assignment.

The two-person team traveled to Uganda, where they planted themselves in various rural communities and in the capital city of Kampala, where they talked to local women about the on-the-ground realities of microfinance. In the course of their fieldwork, the pair noted an acute need for keeping accurate records of financial transactions but also saw the obstacles of doing so with the tools and technologies we take for granted in the West. The use of electronics is not widespread in rural Africa. Components need to be simple and robust. Products need to be designed so that they may be easily repaired or inexpensively replaced. Reprogramming a Windows-like interface is far too costly for the small populations of tribes speaking numerous languages and dialects. The closer the team looked, the more daunting the list of constraints became.

With the return of the field researchers, the full design team began work on a product that owed more to IDEO's decades-long work with the toy industry than with consumer electronics. The device uses simple, off-the-shelf electronic components that are inexpensive, readily available, and easy to repair. Instead of an interface based on a large, expensive display, a simple printed-paper keyboard sits over the buttons so that adapting to a new language is as simple as printing a new piece of paper—or even handwriting a new sheet. The "Universal Remote Transaction Device" would not have been a big hit at the annual International Consumer Electronics Show in Las Vegas, but it was an appropriate tool for an emerging market in a developing country. Even better, the device could be used not just for keeping track of microfinancial transactions but also for remote monitoring of health care incidents, agricultural issues, supply-chain management, and more.

I wrote early on about the benefits that come from seeking out extreme users and why the most compelling insights often come from looking outward, to the edges of the market. The objective is not so much to design for these marginal, outlying populations as to gain inspiration from their passion, their knowledge, or simply the extremity of their circumstances. We may, however, be far too timid about what this concept implies. Even when we look at tech-savvy teenagers in Korea to help us think about what's next for middle-aged Americans, we are sticking to the places and people we already know and to consumer-oriented problems that are basically our own. We do not often think of going to the poorest, most neglected corners of the earth to learn about the lives of people who have fallen out of the system, but this is where we may find globally applicable solutions to the world's most pressing problems. Sometimes necessity is the mother of innovation.

This argument can be misconstrued. Though it is praiseworthy to contribute our talents to the eradication of preventable disease, disaster relief, and rural education, too often our instinct has been to think of these interventions as social acts that are different from and superior to the practical concerns of business. They are the domain of foundations, charities, volunteers, and NGOs, not of "soulless corporations," which attend only to the bottom line. Neither of these is any longer an acceptable model, however. Businesses that focus solely on bumping up their market share by a few tenths of a percentage point miss significant opportunities to change the rules of the game, and nonprofit organizations that go it alone may be denying themselves access to the human and technical resources necessary to create sustainable, systemic long-term change. The influential business strategist C. K. Prahalad has written about the fortune to be found at the "bottom of the pyramid" by companies that dare to approach the world's poorest citizens not as suppliers of cheap labor or recipients of their charitable largesse but rather as partners in creative entrepreneurship. Prahalad's description of the Aravind Eye Hospital in Madurai, India, is a case in point.

## a passage to India

Aravind was founded in 1976 by the late Dr. G. Venkataswamy—"Dr. V," as everyone called him—to explore ways to deliver medical care to inhabitants of poor and developing countries. The alternatives, at that time, were to import practices and facilities from the West—which placed them impossibly beyond the reach of most Indians—or to rely on "traditional" practices, which deny people the fruits of modern research and often simply mean no treatment at all. Dr. V felt there must be a third way.

My own passage to India began with a visit to one of Aravind's mobile eye camps in the "suburbs" of Madurai in the southern Indian state of Tamil Nadu. I didn't expect neat, three-bedroom houses in planned communities. On the other hand, I was not prepared for what I saw: shantytowns cobbled together out of cardboard boxes and corrugated metal, simple houses mixed with workshops left over from the Raj, shops the size of a Wal-Mart parking space selling every imaginable necessity. But I also saw people having their eyes tested. I saw how more complex cases were transmitted via satellite back to the hospital, where experienced doctors could make the final diagnosis. I watched patients with operable cataracts boarding a bus headed for Aravind, where they would have the operation the same day.

Aravind has its own in-house manufacturing facility that makes the intraocular lenses and sutures used in cataract operations. It is an amazing example of the use of extreme constraints as the inspiration for breakthrough innovation. Dr. David Green, who has been honored by the Ashoka Foundation, the MacArthur Foundation, and the Schwab Foundation for Social Entrepreneurship, working with Dr. P. Balakrishnan at Aravind, hypothesized that it might be possible to use small-scale computer-aided manufacturing technology to make the lenses locally rather than importing them from foreign medical suppliers at a cost of approximately $200 per pair. In 1992, through his nonprofit Project Impact, Green set up a small manufacturing unit in the basement of one of the hospitals and started making plastic lenses. Over time it expanded to make sutures as well and ultimately met all the international standards it needed to export products internationally. Aurolab (as they eventually named their basement start-up) is now the biggest exporter of lenses and sutures in the developing world. It has recently relocated to a new factory. A confessed "serial social entrepreneur," Green has turned his attention to hearing loss and pediatric AIDS drugs—a global campaign that started as a prototype within the Aravind system.

In the hospital itself we dressed in scrubs and toured the wards, where physicians perform more than 250,000 surgeries per year. Assembly-line operating procedures are at the core of Aravind's productivity. As a surgeon removed the damaged lens from one patient in a quick but skillful procedure, the next patient was being prepared right alongside in the operating room. Postoperative recovery did not take place in a fancy ward with satellite TV and cut flowers but in a simple room with rush mats on the floor, where patients spent the night before returning home the next day. It was not luxurious by the standards of the West, but it was as comfortable as the beds they slept in at home. For about a third of the patients it was free; the remainder paid on a sliding scale, which began at 3,000 rupees (about $65) and for which they received exactly the same care.

It is unlikely that a Western doctor, hospital administrator, architect, or industrial designer would have forgone expensive wards in favor of rush mats and concrete floors, even if their mission were to help the blind. This insight grew out of Dr. V's empathy with the culture of the poor. He realized that giving his patients something consistent with what they were accustomed to in their villages but still good enough to meet acceptable medical standards, allowed him to serve the poor in an economically viable way. And he has succeeded. The Aravind Eye Hospital has served millions of patients. Aurolab operates at a 30 percent profit, which is plowed back into clinics in Nepal, Egypt, Malawi, and Central America. While the Aravind management team takes private donations to fund additional work, the operating model is self-sustaining and the clinic is no more reliant on charitable donations than the majority of Western health care facilities.

Although many people have praised Aravind for its entrepreneurial model of "compassionate capitalism," as a designer my experience there showed me the enormous potential of working under extreme constraints. How ironic that the holy grail of corporate America—where innovation leads to breakthrough solutions and enhanced profitability—should be realized on the straw mats of an eye clinic in rural India. Not only is Aravind providing untold benefits to the citizens of Madurai, Pondicherry, and the other cities in which its hospitals now operate, it is also exporting its ideas and approaches to other health care facilities throughout the developing world—and perhaps beyond. Indeed, there are signs that Aravind's approach, and that of others like it, may become accepted practice in the West. Not only are young surgeons coming from the United States and Europe to train at Aravind, patients too are beginning to travel to India in search of world-class care at a fraction of the price they would pay in New York or Los Angeles.

Dr. Venkataswamy died in 2006. To the end of his life, when he spoke about his vision for Aravind he liked to use McDonald's as the standard of scale and efficiency that he dreamed of bringing to health care. His achievement was to use the design thinker's tools of empathy, experimentation, and prototyping to reach McDonald's-like efficiency in an organic, sustainable way.

# food for thought

A thousand miles to the north, on the outskirts of New Delhi, lies the demonstration farm set up by International Development Enterprises (IDE), India. Founded by the social entrepreneur Paul Polak, IDE's mission is to provide low-cost solutions that meet the needs of small farmers in developing countries. The narrow road that leads to the farm passes through fields of healthy crops irrigated by a variety of techniques. In one corner there are drip irrigation pipes, in another sprinklers made from very simple, low-cost materials. Amitabha Sadangi, who heads IDE (India), repeats the same message over and over: designing for the poor begins and ends with a focus on cost. Every detail must be designed to be no more expensive than necessary, and no efficiency is too small not to seize. This approach would seem sensible to most western manufacturers, but Sadangi and Polak take it one step further. In a rural twist on the quarterly bottom line, they require that any investment made by a farmer be repaid many times over in just one growing season. Whereas an American farmer may take out a loan to buy a hundred-thousand-dollar tractor and repay it over many years, farmers in the developing world cannot take the risk, nor do they have the capital to make such investments. This constraint has led to innovations that have the potential to transform agriculture in the developing world—and perhaps beyond.

Many of IDE's drip irrigation products are designed to last not a decade or two, as we might expect in the West, but for only one or two seasons. This seemingly shortsighted approach may seem irresponsible to a Western engineer, but by using less durable and therefore less expensive materials, IDE has brought the cost of irrigation down to approximately five dollars for a 20-meter-square (67-foot-square) plot of land. A farmer can expect to reap many times this amount in extra profit by growing fruit or vegetables, which will enable him to irrigate more land in future seasons. By driving the cost down, IDE enables farmers to reinvest the additional profits to reach economic sustainability faster and with less risk. And by thus increasing demand for its low-cost systems, IDE, like Aravind, operates on the basis of a sustainable business model.

This approach has the potential to make a significant difference to subsistence farmers in India, Africa, and beyond, but its potential impact may be greater than that. The idea of designing products in an integrated manner such that low cost, entry-level offerings create wealth quickly for customers has applications well beyond farming. In the developing world this business model is being applied to mobile computing, communications services, clean water delivery, rural health care, and affordable housing. Why could it not apply to many of the same sectors in the West? The economic convulsions rocking the developed world as I write suggest that the prevailing model is not working. There could be no more opportune moment to imagine how we might move in the direction of a society where what we buy helps create wealth rather than just consume it. The idea of designing products, services, and business models that create a rapid return on investment seems very attractive, and it is no accident that it first appeared in places where most people have no choice.

Organizations such as the Aravind Eye Hospital, International Development Enterprises, and many others like them are experimenting with approaches that measure success not by profit but by social impact, and they challenge us to think about how these lessons might be applied elsewhere. In one sense, we have seen this kind of innovation before. Toyota, Honda, and Nissan all began their meteoric rise by creating inexpensive solutions for their own markets at a time when Detroit measured the success of its cars by the height of their tailfins. They went on to demonstrate to the world that there is nothing intrinsically "Japanese" about good design, efficient manufacturing, reduced fuel consumption, and low cost. Might the Aravind model not "bounce back" to show us all the way forward? The argument for working with the most extreme users, where the constraints are unforgiving and the cost of failure high, is not just a social one. It may be how we will spot opportunities that have global relevance and how we will avoid becoming the victims of the new competitors who thrive in environments where more prudent organizations fear to tread.

## whom to work with

Whether or not they have adopted or even heard of "design thinking," many of these social entrepreneurs are applying its tenets. Social issues are, by definition, human-centered. The best of the world's foundations, aid organizations, and NGOs know this, but many of them have lacked the tools to ground this commitment in ongoing, sustainable enterprises fueled not just by outside donations but by the energies and resources of the people they serve.

In 2001 Jacqueline Novogratz created Acumen Fund, a New York–based social venture fund that invests in enterprises in East Africa and South Asia committed to serving the poor in an ongoing and sustainable way. Acumen has invested in both for profit and not-for-profit enterprises ranging from franchised health clinics to affordable housing. Its model is gaining worldwide attention. Novogratz has spoken explicitly about how her leadership team used design thinking—in addition to the standard metrics of investment "performance"—to evaluate the success of individual investments based on a balance of business sustainability and social impact. Indeed, our shared interest in using design thinking to balance business goals with philanthropic objectives has led IDEO into an ongoing partnership with Acumen Fund.

Our collaboration began with a series of workshops in which we explored a set of critical needs that might be translated into viable projects, ranging from antimalarial bed nets to hygiene and sanitation. We decided to focus on clean water. In the developing world, some 1.2 billion people are at risk of disease from drinking unsafe water. Even when water is collected from a high-quality source, it often becomes contaminated during the lengthy trip, often by foot and usually over bad roads, to its final destination. The team drew up its own brief: how might we create safe and easy means of water storage and transportation that improve the health and living conditions of low-income communities while creating opportunities for local entrepreneurs?

As the project progressed, we gathered as many insights into how to implement our ideas as into solutions themselves. No matter how compelling an idea might be, it is of little value if it cannot be sustained by its intended customers in India or Africa. To achieve this, the project team tapped into what the anthropologist Clifford Geertz called the "local knowledge" of NGOs and entrepreneurs in the field, which resulted in numerous culturally appropriate ideas: new types of payment using mobile phones or prepaid coupons, better branding of delivery vehicles to spread awareness, local delivery depots that could be owned and run by the community. Future steps will focus on ways to support these local groups as they bring ideas to market.

Aravind, IDE, and Acumen Fund offer examples not just of well-designed products but of design thinking applied across the entire spectrum of a problem: the product, the service in which the product is embedded, the business model of the enterprise that provides the service, the investors behind the enterprise, and more. It is a mistake to think of them as organizations of well-intentioned, well-heeled do-gooders. These social enterprises have set out to achieve the integration of the desirability-viability-feasibility triad. This has naturally led to cross-disciplinary initiatives. In Aravind's case most of the design thinkers involved were doctors, not designers. The design thinkers at the Acumen Fund are venture capitalists and development experts. They have learned to maneuver their way through government bureaucracies and adapt their efforts to available infrastructure because systemic problems can be addressed only through systemwide collaboration.

## what to work on

In contrast to companies that may be struggling to extend their brands into a new subniche of a saturated market, the opportunities for socially engaged design are everywhere. Indeed, that is itself a problem, at least while there is a limited amount of design thinking talent to go around. The Rockefeller Foundation recently asked IDEO to consider how the design industry might make a greater contribution to solving social problems. After talking to dozens of NGOs, foundations, consultants, and designers, one of our most telling insights was that our efforts are in danger of being spread far too thinly. There are ten potential projects for every design thinker with the time and the talent to tackle them, and 95 percent of them are in Africa, Asia, and Latin America—which complicates the challenge of getting out into the field to gain insight or quickly and iteratively prototype our ideas.

The solution is to find some way to aggregate the efforts of design thinkers globally so as to create a critical mass, build momentum, and begin to make real progress on some of the selected problems we want to address. One of the most promising examples of this is the charitable organization Architecture for Humanity, cofounded in 1999 by Cameron Sinclair. In its first iteration Sinclair used the Web to bring architectural talent to bear on the design of emergency housing and shelters in response to major disasters such as the 2004 tsunami that devastated Southeast Asia and Hurricane Katrina in the following year. A TED prize enabled him to create the Open Architecture Network, which provides a platform for tackling longer-range, systemic issues, not just responding to ad hoc emergencies. The network's modest mission is to "improve the living standards of five billion people" by setting design challenges, posting design solutions so that they can be shared and improved, connecting stakeholders, and creating a participative approach to solving design problems. It seeks, in effect, to leverage the collective energies of architects and designers worldwide in a way that aggregates, focuses, and amplifies them.

If we need to set priorities, the United Nations' Millennium Development Goals would be a good place to start, but "eradicating extreme poverty" and "promoting gender equality" are far too broad to serve as effective design briefs. If the Millennium Development Goals are to be met, they will have to be translated into practical design briefs that recognize constraints and establish metrics for success. More promising questions might be:

*How might we enable poor farmers to increase the productivity of their land through simple, low-cost products and services?*

*How might we enable adolescent girls to become empowered and productive members of their community through better education and access to services?*

*How might we train and support community health workers in rural communities?*

*How might we find low-cost alternatives to wood-burning and kerosene stoves in urban slums?*

*How might we create an infant incubator that does not need an electrical supply?*

The key, as every designer knows, is to craft a brief with enough flexibility to release the imagination of the team, while providing enough specificity to ground its ideas in the lives of their intended beneficiaries.

## sometimes the thing to do is stay home

Not all the most critical social design issues are to be found in the developing world. Western health care—to take what is only the most obvious example—is facing an imminent crisis. Indeed, for many millions of Americans the system has already broken down. Rising costs are threatening the stability of the system, while as a society we have committed ourselves to unhealthy lifestyles that exact a tremendous social and economic toll. Medical researchers focus their energies on cures for chronic diseases—heart disease, cancer, stroke, diabetes—and policy experts work to improve the efficiency of health care administration and delivery. In isolation, however, these efforts will never be sufficient. A sustained effort to integrate these paths and explore divergent alternatives is needed, and this is where design thinking can help.

In medicine, once the patient has been stabilized, the larger task is to identify the source of the condition—to move as it were, from the *curative* to the *preventive* side of the problem. A case in point is obesity, which contributes to several of the leading causes of death in Western society and is now clinically described as having reached epidemic proportions. Some of the relevant factors relate to a person's biological, cultural, demographic, and geographic circumstances, while others lie within the domain of personal choice. All of them present opportunities for design thinking.

The incidence of childhood obesity has skyrocketed in recent decades; according to the Centers for Disease Control and Prevention, the number of overweight and obese children has tripled since 1980. What used to be called adult-onset diabetes has had to be renamed type 2 diabetes because it is no longer just adults who get it and it is no longer unusual to see kids taking insulin. At the individual level we might start by thinking about why kids develop poor eating habits early in life that are difficult to change later on. We can then begin to think about ways to address some of those issues. Some school districts have banned junk food in cafeterias and vending machines, but simply depriving kids of food they want is self-defeating. More promising are positive inducements such as that of Alice Waters, the founder of the renowned Berkeley restaurant Chez Panisse. Waters has started an initiative called Edible Schoolyard to encourage schools to grow produce to provide healthy ingredients for school lunches while educating kids about where their food comes from. In the United Kingdom, Jamie Oliver developed his School Dinners program, which works with local authorities to introduce healthier, better-tasting food. Each of these can be thought of as the response to a classic design challenge. Instead of the Millennium Development Goals' righteous exhortation to "end childhood obesity," they are asking the design thinker's question: "How might we . . . encourage kids to eat healthier foods?"

The other half of the obesity equation has to do with fitness and exercise—what both economists and nutritionists might agree to call an "input-output" model. While we consume more calories than ever, ours may be the least active generation in history. Here, too, lie opportunities for design thinking to contribute to what has typically been considered either a medical or a public policy issue. Nike, for instance, has mobilized its internal design teams to help them not just to *provide equipment to athletes* but to *learn about their behaviors.* This has in turn led to some significant product innovations. Since 2006 Nike's customers have tracked more than 100 million miles using a simple device that sits inside their running shoes and communicates data about their pace and distance to their iPods. On arriving home, they download the data to a Web site where they can review their progress over time or against that of fellow runners. Nike's innovation is to close the information loop by allowing people to evaluate the effects of their behavior. The Wii Fit from Nintendo similarly taps into people's need to see results but—alas—without having to leave the comfort of their living rooms.

These first small steps toward encouraging healthier behaviors will have to be repeated countless times before significant societal benefit is realized, but they do indicate that there is hope. Design thinkers have become adept at approaching important social issues from the angle of individual motivations and the behaviors that follow, but there is also a level of analysis that needs to be directed at the social forces that constrain the choices we are able to make in the first place. Healthy bodies are a necessary but not sufficient condition of a healthy society, but the reverse is also true. Around the world, design thinkers have become activists and are applying their skills to sources of social dysfunction.

## from global to local

The British Council for Industrial Design was formed at the end of World War II to assist in postwar economic recovery, but since that time it has broadened its mission to the application of design to a diverse range of contemporary social issues. In recent years the Design Council, as it is now known, has collaborated with national and local authorities to bring creative problem solving to bear on questions that could scarcely have been imagined a decade ago. In "Dott 07 (Designs of the Times)," the Council sponsored a year of community-based projects, competitions, exhibitions, conferences, symposia, and festivals throughout northeast England to explore such questions as "Can design help in the fight against crime?" "Are our food production systems ripe for a redesign?" "How can design make schools more sustainable?" One particularly successful program, Design and Sexual Health (DASH) set out to balance the requirements of publicity and discretion in encouraging people to take advantage of a social service that typically carries a stigma. The project team first surveyed 1,200 residents, community leaders, and health professionals and then went on to create an integrated program of communication, education, and clinic and service design that focused not on diseases but on the experience of visitors to the clinics.

Hilary Cottam, herself a onetime director of the Design Council, has taken this approach to local design thinking one step further. Teaming up with the innovation expert Charles Leadbeater and the digital entrepreneur Hugo Manassei, she created Participle, an organization dedicated to creating new social solutions through the collaboration of local communities and leading experts from around the world. Taking a design-led approach and basing its work on the philosophies of the British welfare state first established by Sir William Beveridge, the team at Participle has tackled issues ranging from loneliness in old age to improving the integration of youth into society. One project, called Southwark Circle, resulted in a new membership organization that helps the aged take care of household tasks. Ideas were refined and prototyped in collaboration with older people and their families before the service was launched in Southwark, South London, in early 2009. Cottam believes that locally created solutions can ultimately lead to national models for community-based social services.

## designing future design thinkers

Perhaps the most important opportunity for long-term impact is through education. Designers have learned some powerful methods for arriving at innovative solutions. How might we use those methods not just to educate the next generation of designers but to think about how education as such might be reinvented to unlock the vast reservoir of human creative potential?

In 2008 I spoke to students at the Art Center College of Design in Pasadena about "Serious Play," the connection between the activities we all participated in as children and the characteristics of innovation and creativity. I argued that exploring the world with our hands, testing out ideas by building them, role playing, and countless other activities are all natural characteristics of children at play. By the time we enter the adult world, however, we have lost most of these precious talents. The first place this begins to happen is at school. The focus on analytical and convergent thinking in education is so dominant that most students leave school with the belief either that creativity is unimportant or that it is the privilege of a few talented oddballs.

Our objective, when it comes to the application of design thinking in schools, must be to develop an educational experience that does not eradicate children's natural inclination to experiment and create but rather encourages and amplifies it. As a society our future capacity for innovation depends on having many more people literate in the holistic principles of design thinking, just as our technological prowess depends on having high levels of literacy in math and science. Surprisingly, perhaps, for a firm that won its reputation doing industrial design for the likes of Apple, Samsung, and Hewlett-Packard, engagements with public and private schools, with the educational initiatives of groups such as the W. K. Kellogg Foundation, and with colleges and universities has become a growing part of IDEO's work.

Ormondale is a public elementary school in the affluent Bay Area community of Portola Valley. The school's staff had become convinced that "in order to produce 21st century learners, we could not use 18th century methods." In contrast to the expectations of our corporate clients, Ormondale asked us not to deliver a finished design but rather to facilitate a process in which those designing the program—the teachers themselves—would be responsible for implementing it. The team brainstormed, led workshops, developed curricular prototypes, and conducted observations of analogous institutions ranging from a wildlife conservation network to a Mormon food distribution network. The Ormondale teachers have now developed a set of tools based on a shared philosophy of "investigative learning" that engages students as seekers of knowledge rather than receivers of information. The process—participatory design—mirrored the end product: a participatory teaching and learning environment.

Opportunities to rethink the structure of education exist all the way up the chain. Within the structure of a traditional art school, the California College of the Arts in San Francisco has applied the principles of design thinking—user-centered research, brainstorming, analogous observations, prototyping—to crafting its strategic plan for the future of arts education. The Royal College of Art in London is collaborating with its neighbor, the Imperial College, to leverage the different but mutually reinforcing types of creative problem solving found in art and engineering. In Toronto students at the Ontario College of Art & Design have the opportunity to team up with their counterparts at UT's Rotman School of Management in a shared pursuit of creativity and innovation.

One of the newest experiments can be found at Stanford University in the Hasso Plattner Institute of Design—the so-called d-School. The d-School does not seek to educate traditional designers and does not, in fact, offer any "design" courses at all. Rather, it serves as a unique environment where graduate students in fields as far flung as medicine, business, law, and engineering can come together to work on collaborative design projects in the public interest. The d-School encourages human-centered research, brainstorming, and prototyping in every student project, but it also applies these core principles of design thinking to itself. Spaces are fungible, academic ranks are irrelevant, the curriculum is in permanent flux—it is, in short, an ongoing prototype of the educational process itself.

Finding ways to apply the principles of design thinking to

the problems of society—on the outskirts of Kampala, in the offices of a social venture fund in New York, or in the classrooms of an elementary school in California—is the sort of problem that is attracting the most ambitious designers, entrepreneurs, and students today. They are motivated not by an altruistic desire to "give something back" for a few months after graduation or upon retirement but by the fact that the greatest challenges are always the source of the greatest opportunities.

The projects and personalities highlighted in this chapter are about not charity, philanthropy, or self-sacrifice but a genuine reciprocity of interests. There is nothing wrong with "stopping out" for a year or two to help the Peace Corps build a playground in Nepal or El Salvador. The initiatives examined here, however, do not call for highly trained specialists to *interrupt* their careers but for them to *redirect* them in ways that serve those in extreme need.

If we are to build on one another's good ideas—one of the key tenets of design thinking—we will, at least for the time being, have to focus on a finite set of problems so that our successes can be cumulative over time and place. This begins with nurturing the natural creativity of all children and keeping it alive as they advance through the educational system and into professional life. There is no better way to fill the pipeline with tomorrow's design thinkers.

# designing tomorrow—*today*

I t would be tempting to end this book on the inspiring theme of how design thinking can not only contribute to the success of companies but also promote the general welfare of humanity. The people and projects described in the previous pages are at the leading edge of design thinking. They show what is possible when people tackle the right problems and are committed to seeing them through to their logical conclusions. But, to steal a phrase from Stanford professors Jeffrey Pfeffer and Bob Sutton, design thinking requires bridging the "knowing-doing gap." The tools of the design thinker—getting out into the world to be inspired by people, using prototyping to learn with our hands, creating stories to share our ideas, joining forces with people from other disciplines—are ways of deepening what we know and widening the impact of what we do.

Throughout this book, I have tried to show not only how the designer's skills can indeed be applied to a wide range of problems but also that these skills are not innate and are accessible to a far greater range of people than may be commonly supposed. These two threads come together when we apply them to one of the most challenging problems of them all: designing a life.

## getting started

Design thinking evolved from humble beginnings: crafts-men such as William Morris, architects such as Frank Lloyd Wright, industrial designers such as Henry Dreyfuss and Ray and Charles Eames aspired to make the world around us more accessible, more beautiful, and more meaningful. The complexity and sophistication of the discipline grew over time as designers sought to systematize and generalize what they did.

It is difficult to classify the design thinkers we have met throughout this book according to a simple formula. Although we tend to see people as either thinkers or doers, analyzers or synthesizers, right-brain artists or left-brain engineers, we are whole people, and characteristics emerge when we are put into the right situation. When I left art school, I saw design as a deeply personal art. I certainly did not worry about its connection with business, engineering, or marketing. Once I entered the real world of professional practice, however, I found myself immersed in projects whose interdisciplinary complexity reflected the world around me and began to discover aptitudes I'd never known I had. I'm convinced that given the opportunity—and the challenge—most people will have the same experience and will be able to apply the integrative, holistic skills of the design thinker to business, society, and life.

## DESIGN THINKING AND YOUR ORGANIZATION

### begin at the beginning

Design thinking starts with divergence, the deliberate attempt to expand the range of options rather than narrow them. The designer's inclination to explore new directions is of little value if it comes at the end of the innovation process, by which time the arc of the story has begun to close. Companies should have design thinkers sitting on their corporate boards, participating in their strategic marketing decisions, and taking part in the early stages of their R&D efforts. They will bring the capacity to create new unexpected ideas and will use the tools of design thinking as a means of exploring strategy. Design thinkers will connect the upstream with the downstream.

### take a human-centered approach

Because design thinking balances the perspectives of users, technology, and business, it is by its nature integrative. As a starting point, however, it privileges the intended user, which is why I have consistently referred to it as a "human-centered" approach to innovation. Design thinkers observe how people behave, how the context of their experience affects their reaction to products and services. They take into account the emotional meaning of things as well as their functional performance. From this try to identify people's unstated, or latent, needs and translate them into opportunities. The human-centered approach of the design thinker can inform new offerings and increase the likelihood of their acceptance by connecting them to existing behaviors. Asking the right kinds of questions often determines the success of a new product or service: Does it meet the needs of its target population? Does it create meaning as well as value? Does it inspire a new behavior that will be forever associated with it? Does it create a tipping point?

The typical default approach is to start with prevailing business constraints—marketing budgets, supply-chain networks, and the like—and extrapolate from there, but this tactic leads to incremental ideas that are easily copied. Starting with technology is the second most common approach but is risky and best left to agile start-ups that are in a position to bet on something new and untested. Starting with humans increases the likelihood of developing a breakthrough idea and finding a receptive market—whether managers of fancy resort hotels or subsistence farmers in Cambodia. At both extremes, the first step is to ensure that those involved in your innovation efforts get as close as they can to their intended customers. Reams of market data are no substitute for getting out into the world.

## fail early, fail often

Time to first prototype is a good measure of the vitality of an innovation culture. How rapidly are ideas made tangible so that they can be tested and improved? Leaders should encourage experimentation and accept that there is nothing wrong with failure as long as it happens early and becomes a source of learning. A vibrant design-thinking culture will encourage prototyping—quick, cheap, and dirty—as part of the creative process and not just as a way of validating finished ideas. A promising prototype will generate a buzz among members of the design team, who will become enthusiastic advocates as it becomes a candidate for funding and support. The real test of a prototype, however, is not internal but out in the world, where it can be experienced by the farmers, schoolchildren, business travelers, or surgeons who are its intended users. Prototypes need to be testable, but they do not need to be physical. Storyboards, scenarios, movies, and even improvised acting can produce highly successful prototypes—the more the better.

## get professional help

I do not cut my own hair or change the oil in my car, even though I probably could. There are times when it makes more sense to go outside your organization and look for opportunities to expand the innovation ecosystem. Sometimes this will take the form of cocreation with customers or new partners. Sometimes it will mean hiring experts, who may be technology specialists, software geeks, design consultants, or fourteen-year-old video gamers. We have seen how, with the help of the Internet, products and services are moving beyond passive consumption. The active participation of customers and partners is not only likely to yield more ideas but will create a web of loyalty that will be hard for your competitors to erode. Innovators will exploit Web 2.0 networks to expand the effective scale of their teams, and hyperinnovators will be ready for 3.0 whenever it comes.

Extreme users are often the key to inspirational insights. These are the specialists, the aficionados, and the outright fanatics who experience the world in unexpected ways. They force us to project our thinking to the edges of our existing customer base and expose issues that would otherwise be disguised. Seek out extreme users and think of them as a creative asset. Remember that they may be found on the other side of town or the other side of the world.

## share the inspiration

Don't forget your internal network. Much of the effort concerning knowledge sharing over the past decade has been focused on efficiency. It may be time to think about how your knowledge networks support *inspiration*—not just streamlining the progress of existing programs but stimulating the emergence of new ideas. How can you connect like-minded folks to leverage their common passions? What is the typical fate of new ideas within your organization? How can you leverage insights about consumers to inspire multiple projects? Are you using digital tools to document your project outcomes in a way that deepens the knowledge base of your organization and allows individuals to learn from it and to grow?

The rise of virtual collaboration—and of airfares—makes it easy to forget the value of bringing people together in the same room. In a hundred years this notion may seem quaint, but for now it is the way to create powerful bonds. Challenge your organization to think about how it can spend more time doing collaborative, generative work that will produce a tangible outcome at the end of the day—not having more meetings. Face-to-face time cultivates relationships and nourishes teams and is one of the most precious resources an organization possesses. Make it as productive and creative as possible. Building on the ideas of others is a whole lot easier when the building is happening in real time and among people who know and trust one another. And it is usually a whole lot more fun.

## blend big and small projects

There is no silver bullet for innovation. Think of it more as "silver buckshot." It makes sense to take a variety of approaches to innovation, but think about which ones are most likely to leverage the strengths of your organization. Diversify your assets. Manage a diversified portfolio of innovation that stretches from shorter-term incremental ideas—how to increase the mileage of this year's model—to longer-term revolutionary ones—how to produce a car that runs on soybeans or sunbeams. The majority of your efforts will take place in the incremental zone, but without exploring more revolutionary ideas you risk being blindsided by unexpected competition. The downside: you may see fewer of these projects going to market. The upside: those that do are likely to have a lasting impact.

Encouraging experimentation is easy in the incremental zone. Business units should be encouraged to drive innovation around existing markets and offerings. The creative leader must also be willing to support the search for more breakthrough ideas from the top, whether this means introducing a new line of office furniture or a new primary school curriculum. Most organizations have metrics that measure the effectiveness of a division on its own terms. This type of thinking undermines effective collaboration across departmental silos. It is precisely in the interstitial spaces, however, that the most interesting opportunities lie.

## budget to the pace of innovation

Design thinking is fast-paced, unruly, and disruptive, and it is important to resist the temptation to slow it down by relying on cumbersome budgeting cycles or bureaucratic reporting procedures. Rather than sabotage your most creative asset, be prepared to rethink funding schedules as projects unfold according to their own internal logic and teams learn more about the opportunities before them.

Agile resource allocation is challenging in any organization and downright scary in large ones. But there may be ways around a crippling reliance on the predictability of markets and the discipline of annual budgets. Some companies have experimented with venture funds that can be tapped to support promising projects. Others rely on the judgment of senior management to release funding as projects reach certain milestones. The trick is to accept that milestones cannot be predicted with certainty and that projects acquire an inner life of their own. Budgeting guidelines must be expected to change many times over. The key to agile budgeting is a review process that relies upon the judgment of senior leadership rather than some kind of algorithmic process mechanically applied. That's how venture capital funds operate, and successful venture capitalists are nothing if not nimble.

## find talent any way you can

Design thinkers may be in short supply, but they exist inside every organization. The trick is spotting them, nurturing them, and freeing them to do what they do best. Who among your staff spends time watching and listening to customers? Who would rather build a prototype than write a memo? Who seems to get more out of working with a team than holed up in a tastefully appointed cubicle? Who comes to the organization with a weird background (or just a weird tattoo) that might be a clue to a different way of looking at the world? These people are your raw material and your energy supply. They are money in the bank. And since they are accustomed to being marginalized, they will respond with alacrity to an opportunity to get involved in exciting projects at the earliest stage. If they happen to be designers, get them out of the comfort of their design studio and into interdisciplinary teams. If they are from Accounting, Legal, or HR, give them some art supplies.

Once you have tapped your internal resources, think about how you handle recruiting. Hire budding design thinkers from schools that "get it," and bring in some interns and team them up with the more seasoned design thinkers you already have. Create some projects that have relatively short time horizons but are focused on divergent thinking. Share the results around the organization. Get a buzz going around design thinking, and converts will come crawling out of the woodwork. There is nothing as seductive to a true innovator as optimism.

## design for the cycle

In many organizations the cadence of business calls for people to shift their job assignments every eighteen months or so. However, most design projects take longer to move from the launching pad and through their implementation phase—particularly projects aimed at a real breakthrough. When core team members are not able to follow a project through the complete cycle, both will suffer. The guiding idea behind a project is likely to be diluted, attenuated, or lost. Individuals will feel that their learning curves have been wasted and may be left with a sense of frustration that is hard to shake. The experience of going through the entire cycle of a project is invaluable.

## DESIGN THINKING AND YOU

There is something wondrously gratifying about putting something new out into the world, whether it is an award-winning piece of industrial design, an elegant mathematical proof, or a first poem published in the high school newspaper. Many people find that cultivating this feeling of personal accomplishment is a powerful driving force. It also happens to be sound business practice because it makes us less likely to accept the familiar, the expedient, or the boring.

### don't ask *what?* ask *why?*

Every parent knows how infuriating five-year-olds can be with their constantly questioning "Why?" Every parent has at one point or another retreated behind the authoritarian "Because I said so." For the design thinker, asking "Why?" is an opportunity to reframe a problem, redefine the constraints, and open the field to a more innovative answer. Instead of accepting a given constraint, ask whether this is even the right problem to be solving. Is it really faster cars that we want or better transportation? Televisions with more features or better entertainment? A snazzier hotel lobby or a good night's sleep? A willingness to ask "Why?" will annoy your colleagues in the short run, but in the long run it will improve the chances of spending energy on the right problems. There is nothing more frustrating than coming up with the right answer to the wrong question. This is as true in responding to a brief or designing a new strategy for a company as it is in striking a meaningful balance between work and life.

## open your eyes

We spend most of our lives not noticing the important things. The more familiar we are with a situation, the more we take for granted, which is why it usually takes a visiting relative to get us to visit Alcatraz or the Golden Gate Bridge, or spend a weekend in the Wine Country. My friend Tom Kelley likes to point out that "Innovation begins with an Eye," but I'd like to take this one step further. Good design thinkers observe. Great design thinkers observe the ordinary. Make it a rule that at least once a day you will stop and think about an ordinary situation. Take a second look at some action or artifact that you would look at only once (or not at all) as if you were a police detective at a crime scene. Why are manhole covers round? Why is my teenager heading off to school dressed like that? How do

I know how far back I should stand from the person in front of me in line? What would it be like to be color-blind? If we immerse ourselves in what Naoto Fukasawa and Jasper Morrison have recently called "the Super-Normal," we can gain uncanny insights into the unwritten rules that guide us through life.

## make it visual

Record your observations and ideas visually, even if just as a rough sketch in a notebook or a picture on your camera phone. If you think you can't draw, too bad. Do it anyway. Every designer I know carries a sketch pad the way a doctor carries a stethoscope. These images will become a treasure trove of ideas to refer to and share.

The same is true for the way we develop our ideas. Ludwig Wittgenstein was the most cerebral of twentieth-century philosophers, but his motto was "Don't think. Look." Being visual allows us to look at a problem differently than if we rely only on words or numbers. I found it more useful to visualize this book as a mind map than to draw up an orderly table of contents. It gave me a sense of the whole that I couldn't get from a linear table of contents. The biologist Barbara McClintock used to speak about "a feeling for the organism." Her colleagues stopped ridiculing her "touchy-feely" approach to science when she was awarded the Nobel Prize in Physiology or Medicine. From Al Gore helping us to visualize the melting of the Greenland icecap to the artist Tara Donovan helping us to visualize a million Styrofoam cups, one picture can, as they say, be worth a thousand words. Maybe more.

## build on the ideas of others

Everyone has heard of Moore's Law and Planck's Constant, but we should be suspicious when an idea becomes too closely identified with the person who first thought it up. If an idea becomes a piece of private property, it is likely to grow stale and brittle over time. If it migrates throughout an organization, undergoing continual permutations, combinations, and mutations, it is likely to flourish. Just as habitats need ecological diversity, corporations need a culture of competing ideas. Jazz musicians and improvisational actors have created an art form around their ability to build on the stories being created in real time by their fellow artists. There are a lot of "IDEOisms" floating around our office, but my favorite might be the oft-repeated reminder that "All of us are smarter than any of us."

## demand options

Don't settle for the first good idea that comes into your head or seize the first promising solution presented to you. There are plenty more where they came from. Let a hundred flowers bloom, but then let them cross-pollinate. If you haven't explored lots of options, you haven't diverged enough. Your ideas are likely to be incremental or easy to copy.

This can be a difficult commitment to honor. The pursuit of new options takes time and makes things more complicated, but it is the route to more creative and satisfying solutions. In the meantime, your colleagues may get frustrated and your customers impatient, but they will be happier with the eventual results.

You just have to know when to stop, and that is an art that can be learned but probably cannot be taught. Setting deadlines is one way. Not only will they put an outer limit on the amount of time you take, you will find that you become even more productive as the deadline looms. Curse deadlines all you want, but remember that time can be our most creative constraint.

## balance your portfolio

One of the most satisfying things about thinking like a designer is that the results are tangible. Something new exists at the end of a project that didn't exist before. Remember to document the process as it unfolds (we don't wait for our kids to become finished adults before taking their pictures!). Shoot videos, preserve drawings and sketches, hold on to presentation documents, and find somewhere to store physical prototypes. Assembled as a portfolio, this material will document a process of growth and record the impact of many minds (which can be useful during performance reviews, job interviews, or when you are trying to explain to your kids just what it is that you do). Dennis Boyle, employee number eight at IDEO, has kept every prototype he ever made (we have declined his request to rent an airplane hangar to store them in). It is hard not to feel proud of your contribution when you have a record of it.

## design a life

Design thinking has its origins in the training and the professional practice of designers, but these are principles that can be practiced by everyone and extended to every field of activity. There is a big difference, though, between planning a life, drifting through life, and *designing* a life.

We all know of people who go through life with every step preplanned. They knew which university they would attend, which internship would lead to a successful career, and at what age they will retire. If they falter, they have parents, agents, and life coaches to take up the slack. Unfortunately, this never works (remember the Black Swan?). And anyway, if you know the winner before the start, there's not much point in playing the game.

Like any good design team, we can have a sense of purpose without deluding ourselves that we can predict every outcome in advance, for this is the space of creativity. We can blur the distinction between the final product and the creative process that got us there. Designers work within the constraints of nature and are learning to mimic its elegance, economy, and efficiency, and as citizens and consumers we too can learn to respect the fragile environment that surrounds and sustains us.

Above all, think of life as a prototype. We can conduct experiments, make discoveries, and change our perspectives. We can look for opportunities to turn processes into projects that have tangible outcomes. We can learn how to take joy in the things we create whether they take the form of a fleeting experience or an heirloom that will last for generations. We can learn that reward comes in creation and re-creation, not just in the consumption of the world around us. Active participation in the process of creation is our right and our privilege. We can learn to measure the success of our ideas not by our bank accounts but by their impact on the world.

• • •

I began this book by describing one of my heroes, a man who lived before the profession of design—not to say design thinking—even existed: the Victorian engineer Isambard Kingdom Brunel. As the challenges of the industrial age spread to every field of human endeavor, a parade of bold innovators who would shape the world as they have shaped my own thinking would follow him. We have met many of them along the "reader's journey" that I have tried to construct: William Morris, Frank Lloyd Wright, the American industrial designer Raymond Loewy, and the team of Ray and Charles Eames. What they all shared was optimism, openness to experimentation, a love of storytelling, a need to collaborate, and an instinct to think with their hands—to build, to prototype, and to communicate complex ideas with masterful simplicity. They did not just *do* design, they *lived* design.

The great thinkers to whom I am so deeply indebted are not as they appear in the coffee-table books about the "pioneers," "masters," and "icons" of modern design. They were not minimalist, esoteric members of design's elite priesthood, and they did not wear black turtlenecks. They were creative innovators who could bridge the chasm between thinking and doing because they were passionately committed to the goal of a better life and a better world around them. Today we have an opportunity to take their example and unleash the power of design thinking as a means of exploring new possibilities, creating new choices, and bringing new solutions to the world. In the process we may find that we have made our societies healthier, our businesses more profitable, and our own lives richer, more impactful, and more meaningful.

## ACKNOWLEDGMENTS

To say *Change by Design* was a team effort risks stating the obvious, but the fact remains there were many who made invaluable contributions. Many of the most important insights should be credited to them. All of the errors should be assigned to me.

My silent partner Barry Katz, through his skillful use of words, made me appear more articulate than I really am. I thank him for the many contributions he made to the text and for the considerable time and effort he put into turning my draft manuscript into something ready for public consumption.

My agent, Christy Fletcher, saw the potential of this project and introduced me to the wonderful team at Harper Business, and particularly to editor, Ben Loehnen. I have heard said that the art of book editing is dying out in the rush of modern publishing, but Ben shows that high-quality editing and speed are not mutually exclusive. It has been a delight to work with him.

Others who played essential roles in shepherding the project through to completion include Lew McCreary at *Harvard Business Review*, who edited my original article "Design Thinking"; Sandy Speicher, Ian Groulx, and Katie Clark, who created the cover concept; Peter Macdonald, who illustrated my mind map; publicists Debbe Stern and Mark Fortier, who work diligently to get the message of *Change by Design* out in the world; Scott

Underwood, who made sure I was being factual about IDEO projects; and my assistant, Sally Clark, who somehow managed to get me to the right places at the right time despite my best attempts to foil her plans.

In the course of researching this book I had the pleasure of visiting some wonderful organizations. I would particularly like to thank Pavi Mehta and Thulsi Thulasiraj of Aravind Eye Hospital; David Green; Amitabha Sadangi of IDE India; and Makoto Kakoi and Naoki Ito of Hakuhodo for being so generous with their time and ideas.

I have had the good fortune to spend time with some very smart people who have significantly influenced my thinking. Many of them have been mentioned in the text, but I wish to acknowledge Jacqueline Novagratz, Bruce Nussbaum, Naoto Fukasawa, Gary Hamel, John Thackera, Bob Sutton, Roger Martin, and Claudia Kotchka, because it is to their accomplishments that I owe many of my ideas. I would also like to thank Chris Anderson of TED, who through his wonderful conference has introduced me to countless ideas and people included in *Change by Design*.

At IDEO I would like to thank Whitney Mortimer, Jane Fulton Suri, Paul Bennett, Diego Rodriguez, Fred Dust, and Peter Coughlan for being regular sounding boards for my ideas. But there would be no *Change by Design* without the project contributions of my colleagues at IDEO and our clients, both past and present. They continue to be an endless source of inspiration.

*Change by Design* reflects as much as anything my journey from designer to design thinker. Without the counsel of certain people I would never have made that journey. They include my parents, who gave me the confidence to head off to art school when all my friends were choosing far more promising careers; Bill Moggridge, who took the significant risk of hiring me; David Kelley, who was willing to entrust his company to my leadership; David Strong, who has the patience to run a business alongside a designer who can barely count (never mind use a spreadsheet); and Jim Hackett, whose leadership advice has provided a constant safety net to me and my colleagues.

Finally, and most important, comes the pleasure of thanking my family—Gaynor, Caitlin, and Sophie. Their willingness to tolerate my frequent absences from home and the many weekends spent hunched over my laptop constitute just a small part of the debt of gratitude I owe them.

TIM BROWN
*Palo Alto, California, May 2009*

In the course of *Change by Design* I have mentioned many projects and examples. Some of those are from the broad world of business, innovation, and design, and I have attributed those in the main body of the text. There are many more that come from the direct experiences of my colleagues at IDEO. To keep the stories brief and to the point I have chosen to attribute those projects here. The following list acknowledges the IDEO core team members who participated in the projects and who have been responsible for all the insights and accomplishments I have relied on to support my argument. I thank them.

## Chapter 1

Coasting bikes for Shimano: *David Webster, Dana Cho, Jim Feuhrer, Gerry Harris, Stephen Kim, Bruce MacGregor, Patrice Martin, Nacho Mendez, Anthony Piazza, Aaron Sklar*

Aquaduct for Innovate or Die: *David Janssens, John Lai, Adam Mack, Brian Mason, Eleanor Morgan, Paul Silberschatz*

Mr. Clean MagicReach for Procter & Gamble: *Chris Kurjan, Jerome Goh, Hans-Christoph Haenlein, Gerry Harris, Aaron Henningsgaard, Adrian James, Carla Pienkanagura, Anna Persson, Nina Serpiello, Jim Yurchenco*

Initiative Success Center: the Gym for Procter & Gamble: *Kristian Simsarian, Matt Beebe, Peter Coughlan, Fred Dust, Suzanne Gibbs Howard, Jerome Goh, Ilya Prokopoff*

Stanford Center for Innovations in Learning: *Dana Cho, Fred Dust, Cheri Fraser, Joanne Oliver, Todd Schulte*

## Chapter 2

Get in Shape for Centers for Disease Control and Prevention: *Jacinta Bouwkamp, Hilary Hoeber, Holly Kretschmar, Molly Van Campen, Chris Waugh*

Kitchen gadgets for Zyliss: *Annetta Papadopoulis, Michael Chung, Hans-Christoph Haenlein, Dana Nicholson, Thomas Overthun, Nina Serpiello, Philip Stob, David Webster, Opher Yom-Tov, Jim Yurchenco, Robert Zuchowski*

Ways and Means for Community Builders: *Leslie Witt, Mary Foyder, Tatyana Mamut, Altay Sendil*

Gates-IDE HCD tool kit for the Bill and Melinda Gates Foundation: *Tatyana Mamut, Jessica Hastings, Sandy Speicher*

Transforming care at the bedside for Institute for Healthcare Improvement and Robert Wood Johnson Foundation: *Peter Coughlan, Ilya Prokopoff, Jane Fulton Suri*

DePaul Health Center for SSM Health Care: *Peter Coughlan, Jerome Goh, Fred Dust, Kristian Simsarian*

Bank customer service strategy for Juniper Financial: *Fran Samalionis, Gretchen Addi, Alex Grishaver, Aaron Lipner, Brian Rink, Rebecca Trump, Laura Weiss, Bill Wurz*

Palm V for Palm: *Dennis Boyle, Joost Godee, Elisha Tal*

## Chapter 4

Diego Powered Dissector System for Gyrus ENT: *Andrew Burroughs, Jacob Brauer, Scott Brenneman, Ben Chow, Niels Clausen-Stuck, Deuce Cruse, Thomas Enders, Dickon Isaacs, Tassos Karahalios, Ben Rush, Amy Schwartz*

Mouse for Apple: *Douglas Dayton, David Kelley, Rickson Sun, Jim Yurchenco*

Communications badge for Vocera: *John Bauer, Scott Brenneman, Bruce MacGregor, Thomas Overthun, Adam Prost, Tony Rossetti, Craig Syverson, Steve Takayama, Jeff Weintraub*

Acela for Amtrak: *Dave Privitera, Ilya Prokopoff, Axel Unger, Bill Stewart*

TownePlace Suites for Marriott: *Bryan Walker, Soren DeOrlow, Patrice Martin, Aaron Sevier*

Future Vision for HBO: *Alex Grishaver, Owen Rogers, Dan Bomze*

## Chapter 5

Improved patient-provider service for Mayo Clinic: *Dana Cho, Fred Dust, Ilya Prokopoff*

Keep the Change account service for Bank of America: *Monica Bueno, Fred Dust, Roshi Givechi, Christian Schmidt, Dave Vondle*

Scenography for Ritz-Carlton: *Dana Cho, Roshi Givechi, Amy Leventhal*

## Chapter 6

Compass laptop computer for GRiD Systems: *Bill Moggridge*

Brand Experience for Snap-on: *Paul Bennett, Martin Bone, Owen Rogers*

Mobility platform videos for Intel: *Martin Bone, Michael Chung, Gregory Germe, Arvind Gupta, Danny Stillion, Andre Yousefi*

Strategic vision for California College of the Arts: *Erik Moga, Brianna Cutts, Jeffrey Nebolini*

Blood donor experience for American Red Cross: *Patrice Martin, Monica Bueno, Kingshuk Das, Sara Frisk, Jerome Goh, Diem Ho, Lee Moreau, John Rehm, Beau Trincia*

## Chapter 7

ExV for Nokia: *Davide Agnelli, Katja Battarbee, Jeff Cunningham, Chris Nyffeler, Kristian Simsarian, Robert Suarez, John Tucker*

RoomWizard for Steelcase: *Mat Hunter, Ingrid Baron, Tim Billing, Scott Brenneman, Tim Brown, Phil Davies, Lynda Deakin, Alison Foley, Dick Grant, Patrick Hall, Simon Leach, Dave Littleton, Suzie Stone, Jim Yurchenco*

Nurse knowledge exchange for Kaiser Permanente: *Denise Ho, Ilya Prokopoff*

## Chapter 8

Checkpoint evolution for Transport Security Administration: *Gretchen Wustrack, Jonah Houston, Holly Bybee, David Janssens, Gerry Harris, Caroline Stanculescu, Jon Kaplan, Aaron Shinn, Roshi Givechi, Ashlea Powell, Yuh-Jen Hsiao, Dirk Ahlgrim, Anke Pierik, Carl Anderson, Santiago Prieto, David Haygood, Ted Barber, Judy*

Lee, Stephen Kim, Annie Valdes, Davide Agnelli, Michelle Ha, Nina Wang, Lionel Mohri, Kelly Grant-Rauh, Tiffany Card

Squish Grip toothbrush for Oral-B: *Thomas Overthun*

Identity and packaging for Pangea Organics: *Ian Groulx, Mary Foyder, Amy Leventhal, Kyle McDonald, Christopher Riggs, Philip Stob, Robert Zuchowski*

Shift focus for the U.S. Department of Energy: *Hans-Christoph Haenlein, Emily Bailard, Heather Emerson, Jay Hasbrouck, Adam Reineck, Jeremy Sutherland, Gabriel Trionfi*

## Chapter 9

Global Remote Transaction Device for Hewlett-Packard: *Alexander Grunsteidl, Aaron Sklar, Paul Bradley, Peter Bronk, Mark Harrison, Jane Fulton Suri*

Ripple Effect for Acumen Fund and Bill and Melinda Gates Foundation: *Sally Madsen, Ame Elliott, Holly Kretschmar, Rob Lister, Maria Redin, Aaron Sklar, Caroline Stanculescu, Jocelyn Wyatt*

Strategy for improved early childhood education: *Hilary Carey, Suzanne Gibbs-Howard, Michelle Lee, Aaron Shin, Sandy Speicher, Caroline Stanculescu, Neil Stevenson*

Investigative learning for Ormondale Elementary School: *Hilary Carey, Colleen Cotter, Sandy Speicher*